The Fiery Maelstrom of Freedom

History Nerds

Published by History Nerds, 2022.

THE FIERY MAELSTROM OF FREEDOM

First edition. March 7, 2022.

ISBN: 979-8215866696

Written by History Nerds.

Also by History Nerds

Celtic History
Ireland

Great Wars of the World
World War 1
World War 2
The Napoleonic Wars: One Shot at Glory
The Serbian Revolution: 1804-1835
Peace Won by the Saber: The Crimean War, 1853-1856
The Wars of the Roses

Irish Heroes
Grace O'Malley: The Pirate Queen of Ireland
William Butler Yeats: Nobel Prize Winning Poet
Scáthach
Finn McCool

The History of the Vikings

Vikings
Longships on Restless Seas

The Rise and Fall of Empires
Rome: The Rise and Fall

Standalone
The History of the United Kingdom
The History of Ireland
The History of America
Stalin
The Fiery Maelstrom of Freedom
The History of Scotland
Robert the Bruce
William Wallace: Scotland's Great Freedom Fighter
The History of Wales

Table of Contents

The Fiery Maelstrom of Freedom

The American Civil War, 1861-1865

Introduction

A nation divided is a nation in great jeopardy. When people are at odds, and a singular nation cannot bridge the yawning gap between those differing beliefs, everything is at stake. Freedom, survival, and democracy are placed at risk - and war is often a step away. The devastating civil war that raged in America from 1861 to 1865 is an iconic example of a nation torn apart by opposing views. Many consider this tumultuous war as a focal point of the entire American history - a defining event that shaped the future of the nation as we know it today. Undoubtedly, the American Civil War was bloody and devastating in many ways, and the whirlwind of death took with it many lives - both civilian and military. Arguably, the most important cause of this conflict was *slavery*, a burning topic in America of that era. At the eve of war, some four million people living in America were African-American slaves - a great percentage of the nation's 32 million inhabitants at the time. This practice created great tensions between the opposing parts of America - the North and the South, with the former consisting of states opposed to slavery, and the latter being pro-slavery states. This, alongside several other key differences, quickly led to animosity, and eventually - war.

The American Civil War was brief, but brutal. It swept across much of the North American continent, but especially in the South, where the pro-slavery states made their stand. After roughly four years of vicious combat, the war left some 750,000 soldiers dead, and more than a million casualties in total. Undoubtedly, it was an important, but nonetheless dark period of America's history, and one that remains a focus of heated debate even today - some 157 years later.

In the following book, we will take an unbiased, sideline glimpse into the causes, the events, and the consequences of this civil war, bringing you close to the important socio-political questions of the 1860's America.

"A Nation Divided"
Causes of the American Civil War

Alas, one cannot talk about the American Civil War from a historic point of view without addressing thoroughly the question of slavery. At the time, this unethical practice was commonplace throughout the North American continent, and thus the subject cannot be avoided. Thankfully, the situation today is thoroughly different, and we can now talk about slavery only from a scholarly, historic perspective - as historians have to. Sadly, slavery was present in numerous civilizations and societies, from the dawn of time. From classical antiquity to the Middle Ages, human rights were often neglected, and innocents were enslaved and their identities erased. One of the last places in the world where this practice continued was America. And, as we all know, the slaves that were present in this nation were almost entirely of African background. Ever since the discovery and the exploration of the African continent, the poor inhabitants of this land were taken away as slaves. The Transatlantic slave trade was started as early as the 15th century, when maritime Arab Muslim traders sought new sources of slaves for their own needs. Numerous warring African tribes sold their prisoners of war to the Muslims and the Europeans that arrived at their shores. Those more powerful tribes freely enslaved poorer, nomadic Africans, seeing them as a source of income, and a diminishing of the competition. The Portuguese landowners purchased African slaves to use them for menial labour on their territories. In fact, the largest early slave owners were the Spanish and the Portuguese.

To that end, it was not unexpected to see slavery firmly established in the new and emerging nation that was America. Many of its early families, of both Jewish and European backgrounds, established their wealth and prominence on slavery. In no time, the number of slaves a family owned was a direct reflection of their power and wealth. Still, the history of slavery in America is somewhat poorly documented. The earliest written documents pertaining to slavery can be dated to the colonial period, to 1619, when the English colonists were introduced to the practice of slavery by the Dutch. However, the earliest model was not slavery per se, but a practice known as *indentured servitude*. After an indentured servant would fulfil the duties that were his through contract, they would often be released from their owners. But these liberties were a threat for early Americans, with a high risk of open rebellion. A great example can be dated to 1676, when one Nathaniel Bacon, with a group of ex-servants, led an open revolt against the landowners of Virginia. Following these events, the wealthy families shifted to slavery, seeing it as a safer, cheaper, and more efficient model.

In pre-Civil War America, slaves were an enormous part of the economy. Early on, the cultivation and sale of tobacco was a major success across the nation, particularly in Virginia, in the south. This boom led to the establishment of many new plantations, and with that, the increased need for workforce. The wealthy plantation owners produced tobacco, cotton, and sugar cane, making agriculture a major branch of the American economy. This, of course, was most prevalent in the American South. And in no time, cotton became the number one source of income for all plantation owners in America. With the invention of the so-called "cotton gin" (cotton engine) in 1793, a machine that quickly and easily separates cotton fibres from their seeds, the textile industry saw a major boom. Cotton textiles became highly sought in Europe, and America was ready to export it. As such, cotton became the defining element of the South and its culture. Sadly, however, it also meant that slavery was also one such defining element. So much was cotton a part of Southern identity that a nickname for the region was made popular: *King Cotton*. The cotton industry was also spreading fast: it soon spread as far as Mississippi and Texas, adding these lands to the core of the later-emerging Confederacy.

The numbers related to the cotton industry are a clear indication in its stellar rise to popularity. In 1814 it was documented that the South produced some 146,000 bales of cotton. In the very next year that number was 209,000, and by 1819 it climbed up to an immense 349,000 bales. By the 1840's, the yield of cotton was increased by 60%, and in the 1850's - by almost 100%. Around this time, an incredible 80% of the global cotton production came from the American South. This stellar success of the industry secured a future for slavery.

But slavery was not exclusive to South only. As far as the northern colonies go, slavery was also established - but not in such great measure as it was in the south. The north's increased opposition to slavery began creating the yawning gap between them and the south. With the establishment of the Northwest Ordinance in 1787, this divide was deepened further. This declaration created the Northwest Territories, and abolished slavery in that region. It also established the Ohio River as the new geographic divide between the free states in the north and the slave-owning states in the South. Undoubtedly, the 1787 Northwest Ordinance helped "set the stage" for the American Civil War, deepening the divide and increasing tensions.

Those slaves that were present in the North had more rights, and were cared about. Of course, the different climate of the North was not favorable for the mass plantations and agriculture as in the south. This meant that the north did not have a great need for slaves. Industry was more prevalent in the north, making a stark difference when compared to the south. The "King Cotton", the American South, was based on a plantation culture, and the southern society continued through the decades as rural and conservative, separated from the increasing need for industrialization and urbanization that bloomed in the north. In many ways, the south was an altogether different land than the north - both in its practices and its traditions. By the late 1850's, the south almost had no industry to speak of. There weren't even railroads around this time. Yet even so, the aged model of slave-owning and plantation agriculture made King Cotton immensely rich.

Radical Differences and No Solutions

For decades before the American Civil War, slavery stood in the path of progression as some giant dividing stone. It created a gap in the American society that was present from at least the 1700's, and had no indication of disappearing. Today, historians agree that the slavery was the number one (but not the *only* one) cause of the disunion of the American people. It was a controversial issue at the creation of the Constitution of the United States in 1787, but was left "hanging in the air" at the time, unsettled. As we mentioned, in that same year, slavery was abolished in the parts of the Northwest, separating the Southern states in a way, from the rest of the United States. Following the constitution, as territorial expansion continued at a rapid pace, with new states and territories emerging, the question of slavery continued to pop up repeatedly - always as a conflict. Should the new territories be slave-owning or not was always the number one cause of discontent in politics. Several bills and legislations were brought in hopes of solving the issue, such as the 1820 Missouri Compromise, and the Compromise of 1850. But these had limited success, and could not stave off the ever-increasing threat of war.

By 1804, most - if not all - northern states abolished slavery, either immediately, or gradually. Not one southern state did so. A major movement in the North was established as well, called *Abolitionism*. The abolitionists sought to end slavery in the whole of the United States, opposing slavery and the slave trade on humanitarian grounds. This movement originated in the Colonial Period, amongst the Puritans, who considered owning of slave a morally wrong and sinful practice. In the period between 1830 and 1840, abolitionism was in full swing, and millions of leaflets and pamphlets were spread around, calling for an end of slavery in America.

Still, it is very important that we address the common folk of the era, both in the North and in the South. Sentiments for and against slavery were not universal across the United States. Not everyone in the South, for example, owned slaves. Only the wealthiest landowners made their prominence through slavery, and many lesser families owned just a few slaves. What is more, many poorer and middle class people from the South didn't own slaves at all, living their traditional lives as ever. Still, owners or not, the vast majority of people in the South supported slavery as an institution, clinging firmly to their southern ways and lifestyle. In fact, when the war began, the majority of souther soldiers fought to protect their "homeland" and a traditional Southern society - of which slavery was an integral part. The majority of southerners firmly believed that the abolition of slavery would destroy the economy of the southern states. In the north, however, not everyone was for the abolition of slavery. Many of the northern soldiers were largely indifferent on the matter, with sentiments not having a singular pattern. Nevertheless, a vast majority followed the abolitionist cause, standing firmly with the northern sentiments.

Another of the major causes of the American Civil War was sectionalism: the economic, social, and political differences between the north and the south regions of the United States. In simplest terms, sectionalism is the undeterred loyalty to one's own region of a nation - instead of the loyalty to the nation as a whole. This was exactly what was unfolding in America prior to the war: the north and the south had marked differences in their social structures, customs, traditions, and lifestyles. The two could not find common grounds. This sectionalism had roots as far back as the Colonial period, when early New England colonies like Massachusetts, Connecticut, and Rhode Island differed from Mid-Atlantic colonies such as Delaware, New York, and Pennsylvania, in terms of economy, slavery, and religion. And in the first half of the 19th century, this sectionalism only grew stronger. The North rapidly grew urbanised and industrialised, while the South remained focused on its plantation agriculture that depended on slavery. From an economic point of view, the differences were apparent:

the urban north was busily developing a strong infrastructure of railways, factories, and telegraphs, thus emphasizing the transport of goods and raw materials. The South, however, emphasized on the production and sale of the said goods and raw materials. As such economic differences grew in corresponding states, so did the North and South form as distinct entities of the United States. Still, a manner of unity and co-dependence was present: the north was more developed and attracted great numbers of European immigrants. It also provided financial support to the south, in form of loans for the production of cotton, sugar, tobacco, and similar main products, where the North had the main say in terms of both transportation and sales. However, this made the citizens of the South feel all the more exploited. However, some minor industry work was present in the South also: by the half of the 19th century, the cotton that was produced in the South constituted some 50% of the entire export of the United States.

Furthermore, the percentage between educated and literate people in these regions differed greatly. In general, Northerners had a higher percentage of educated people, which in turn meant that new and radical progressive ideas were received more open-heartedly. In comparison to this, the South - much more traditional and rural - protected its own beliefs and aspirations, actively fighting against any new movements and ideas. To add to this, the southerners also disliked the urban and industrial progression of the North, sticking to their agrarian lifestyle. But even so, contemporary accounts state that Southerners were more hospitable, kinder, and open-handed than the urban Northerners.

Abolitionism and Mounting Socio-Political Differences

Even greater instability in the United States arose within the American politics, especially with the growing popularity of "Anti-Slavery" politics within the North. This was one of the key catalysts for the tensions that grew out of proportion. The Southerners saw the abolitionist and anti-slavery political movements as a "threat" to their own identity and culture, and provided them with an "enemy". In the period between 1840 and 1850, the abolitionist movement was at an all-time high. The main goal of these diverse abolitionist groups was "unqualified abolition of slavery", and they strove to keep the issue of anti-slavery at the very front of all political matters within the United States. Undoubtedly, the abolitionist currents were the strongest in the area of the early New England Puritan colonies. There, with the strong Puritan heritage, the anti-slavery sentiments were highest. However, in the years preceding the war, the abolitionists and their allies were a movement of liberal reformists who were greatly inspired by the actions of their counterparts in Great Britain. There, the bill to abolish slavery within Great Britain was succesfuly passed in 1833, and showed to the American anti-slavery groups that persistent lobbying, as well as the winning-over of moral and intellectual causes, could bring about the final victory of the Abolitionists. Of course, slavery was not the only issue within the United States that the abolitionists wanted to eradicate. Other socio-economic problems were quite serious as well. These included women's rights, poor education, temperance, alcohol, urbanization, and the need for religious revival.

Several prominent authors and individuals arose as prominent abolitionists and supporters of that cause in the years before the war. Some of these were the noted Massachusetts philosopher and essayist, Henry David Thoreau, his colleague Ralph Waldo Emerson, as well as Theodore Parker - a religious figure - and Frederick Douglass, an ex-slave and one of the leading abolitionists. Furthermore, abolitionist views could be expressed in one of the most radical and popular anti-slavery newspapers of the time, "The Liberator". Both the papers and these leading figures invoked Puritanism and the New England Puritan heritage repeatedly, relying on that religion's moral views.

Another crucial way of spreading the cause of anti-slavery amongst the common folk was the written word. In the North especially, the percentage of literate people was higher, and popular fiction books and novels were increasingly rising in popularity. Through such novels, the abolitionists spread their anti-slavery views and greatly fueled their cause. Most notable of these novels was a popular fiction novel, "Uncle Tom's Cabin", written by Mrs. Harriet Beecher Stowe and published in 1852. The book is often cited as the work that "helped lay the groundwork for the American Civil War". It was an instant bestseller and became the best selling book of the 19th century - beside the Bible. Stowe was a noted abolitionist, and used her novel as a sort of propaganda work, arousing great sentiments amongst the African-Americans and White Americans alike. Another influential work was "Twelve Years a Slave", an alleged slave narrative dictated by an African-American, Samuel Northup, published in 1853. It too became quite popular, stirring the society even further. However, in later years, many noted scholars question the authenticity of the narrative, suggesting that it was largely a work of fiction aimed at furthering the abolitionist cause. Either way, these - and other - novels were a highly successful way of promoting the anti-slavery sentiments amongst he common folk - mostly in the North. Around 1840, the census reveals that around 15,000 people were members of abolitionist societies across America. But by 1855, this number was likely much higher, owing to the rapid spread of the anti-slavery message. In a way, the abolitionists relied on a well-orchestrated propaganda machine - or, if you will, an organized spreading of their message. In churches, in newspapers, fiction novels, conventions, and everywhere else - the immediate and absolute rejection of slavery in the United States was promoted.

Another cause of instability in the United States was a great influx of European Catholic immigrants. Between 1845 and 1854, some three million immigrants came into the United States, looking for a better life. Over one million of these were Irish Catholics. These people were fleeing their homeland due to rampant starvation, due to the so-called "Potato Famine". There is a popular disbelief that the Irish were the most numerous of all immigrants. In fact, the Germans outnumbered them. The Germans exceeded that one million mark, and came to America simply looking for a better life, and not fleeing persecution or famine. Many of them, too, were Catholics. And it was a well-known fact that a great percentage of Germans were already well-to-do, and could buy land in America. This meant that they could settle in various states, and migrate further inland, while the poorer Irish tended to stay in North-eastern cities, such as New York or Chicago. There - due to their poverty - they tended to live in overcrowded tenement buildings and ghettos. In a short time, great tensions arose between the Native-born American citizens and the newly arrived Irish immigrants. The former accused the latter of stealing jobs and causing the wage levels to plummet. The Irish were willing to work for much less, and thus readily took over jobs from generational Americans. The Irish were furthermore associated with rising crime levels and welfare costs. Also prevalent was a widespread fear of a "papal plot to subvert the United States of America" - since almost three million Catholics came into the United States amongst the native Americans who were largely Protestant. In many ways, it was a multi-dimensional change in the American society. The growth of Catholicism was unbelievable: in just four years, from 1850 to 1854, the number of Catholic churches and institutions, as well as clergymen, doubled in size. With that, the political power of these Catholic voters also grew, especially in the North, in New York and Boston. The native-born American citizens, the staunch Protestants, claimed that the Catholic Irish voted en-masse for anyone that their priests or leaders told them to vote for. The Americans saw this as a direct threat to the democracy on which the United States were established. So, we can see that the influx of Catholic European immigrants greatly shook America in the years preceding the Civil War, contributing to the greater instability. The influx brough religious, social, economic, and political changes that could not be reversed once they were set into motion.

Simultaneous to this was the exponential rise of the Republican Party. This party was founded in 1854, following the collapse of the old Whig party, and was formed largely by the opponents of the Kansas-Nebraska Act. This act was brought in 1854, and drafted by the Democratic Senator Stephen Douglas, and allowed a potential expansion of slavery in to the western territories of the United States. The Republican Party was formed as the major anti-slavery political party, and supported classical liberalism and economic reform. It consisted of Northern Protestants, many of whom were businessmen, factory workers, wealthy farmers, professionals, and (following the Civil War), former black slaves. In general, the Republican Party was form as direct opposition to the extension of slavery in America. In 1855, this party had organized members in less than half of the Northern American states, and usually ran third to the Democrats in elections. But less than a year later, the Republican Party gained substantial momentum, progressing from a fledgling coalition into a powerful sectional political party. With this, greater political changes came to America, and the yawning gap between the North and the South was deepened even further.

In May of 1856, three shocking events occurred, two in Washington DC, and one in Kansas. These violent episodes in American pre-Civil War history served to convince many Northerners that the South was a clear and direct threat to their rights and liberties as free Americans. But more importantly, these events served to strengthen the cause of the Republican Party, connecting it with the overall "Northern Cause".

The first event happened on May 8th, 1856, when a southern congressman from Alabama, Philemon Herbert, caused a "dining room melee" when refused service in a Washington DC restaurant. He entered a scuffle with a waiter, and in the end shot him dead. The incident was at once picked up by the Republican Party as a means to spread their message against the South. They printed pamphlets and handbills that portrayed this incident as a direct attack against the honest white workers and farmers, painting the southern slaveholders as disdainful towards "menials" - i.e. the honest northern working class. The Republicans aimed to paint the Southerners as tyrannical slave-owners, repeatedly quoting radical items from the Southern newspapers.

Scandals and Political Tensions

Just two weeks after this incident, on May 22nd 1856, another scandal ensued. This time, it was the "caning" of Senator Charles Sumner of Massachusetts. He was viciously beaten on the Senate floor by a Southern congressman, Preston Brooks. Sumner attacked Brooks with a cane after the latter made a fiery anti-slavery speech, verbally attacking Brooks's first cousin once removed, the South Carolina Senator Andrew Butler. Brooks was beaten nearly to death, and the attack was a major political scandal. Thousands of Northern men and women, Republican sympathizers, were organized into public condemnations of this vicious attack. That very same evening, false news began circulating en-masse of violence erupting in Kansas. False reports arrived from Lawrence, Kansas, which was the center of "free state" anti-slavery settlers, stating that the city was sacked and burned by the pro-slavery militiamen from neighboring Missouri. This quickly grew out of proportion, and the stories soon included rape, murder, and pillaging. However, the truth was much simpler: a brick, falling from a great height, struck and killed a Missouri raider. Kansas was already a sore spot and the cause of much confrontation. It was known as the "Bleeding Kansas", and a source of disputes over slavery. Again, the event served to strengthen the Republican cause, attracting new voters who were previously skeptical. The violence that occurred in May served to strengthen the Republican image of Southern "slave power" and its threat to common folk.

Around this time, the Northern public was furious over the matter, and saw the failure of the Congress, the courts, and the President to exact justice, as a great indignity. A sense of danger prevailed in the society. Of course, the Republican Party quickly took advantage of the situation, and used it as fuel for their propaganda machine - which worked at full speed.

And the Southern press was not idle either. They responded in equal measure, and in May of 1856, Virginia's major newspaper - the Enquirer from Richmond - claimed that the *vulgar abolitionists must be lashed into submission.*" In Alabama, the papers wrote: *"[As a] free society, we sicken at the name ... a conglomeration of greasy mechanics, filthy operatives, small-fisted farmers, and moonstruck theorists ... hardly fit for association with a Southern gentleman's body servant."*

These tensions, of course, caused a great political race in the North. The general public was well aware - thanks to the active propaganda - that the Republican party was ready to "defend their interests against the South". In turn, heated debates and tensions arose over the question of which party was fit to rule. The rise of animosity towards the aged Southern attitudes allowed the Republican Party to attract a wider public to its ranks: both abolitionists and moderates were now willing to vote against the South and its institutions. The anti-slavery sentiment was the unifying link that brought the Republican Party together, allowing it to make great progress in just two years since its creation. On the other side, the Southern slave holders saw this as a big threat. They feared losing the fragile political balance in Congress, which helped protect their interests up to that point.

In 1858, new political changes were ushering America into a new age. In Illinois, two thoroughly different candidates fought for the Senatorial seat. On one side was the seasoned politician Stephen A. Douglas, the Democratic Party candidate, and on the other side was a partial newcomer to the political scene, a former lawyer by the name of Abraham Lincoln - the Republican Party candidate. Both of them competed over a course of two months, engaging in seven debates in order to present to the public their attitudes and goals. This was the period when Abraham Lincoln reached a public audience. Needless to say, the main topics of these debates were the expansion of slavery and racial questions. Arguably the most important debate was held in the city of Freeport in Illinois. Here, Abraham Lincoln sought Douglas' explanation on his decision to support the citizen's right to decide on the legality of slavery within a state. Lincoln wanted to know if the general public was in fact able to completely oust slavery. Douglas replied:

"The next question propounded to me by Mr. Lincoln is, Can the people of a Territory in any lawful way, against the wishes of any citizen of the United States, exclude slavery from their limits prior to the formation of a State constitution? I answer emphatically, as Mr. Lincoln has heard me answer a hundred times from every stump in Illinois, that in my opinion the people of a Territory can, by lawful means, exclude slavery from their limits prior to the formation of a State constitution. Mr Lincoln knew that I had answered that question over and over again. He heard me argue the Nebraska bill on that principle all over the State in 1854, in 1855, and in 1856, and he has no excuse for pretending to be in doubt as to my position on that question. It matters not what way the Supreme Court may hereafter decide as to the abstract question whether slavery may or may not go into a Territory under the Constitution, the people have the lawful means to introduce it or exclude it as they please, for the reason that slavery cannot exist a day or an hour anywhere, unless it is supported by local police regulations. Those police regulations can only be established by the local legislature; and if the people are opposed to slavery, they will elect representatives to that body who will by unfriendly legislation effectually prevent the introduction of it into their midst. If, on the contrary, they are for it, their legislation will favor its extension. Hence, no matter what the decision of the Supreme Court may be on that abstract question, still the right of the people to make a Slave Territory or a Free Territory is perfect and complete under the Nebraska bill. I hope Mr. Lincoln deems my answer satisfactory on that point."

Douglas thus stayed true to his own views and replied that it were the people that decide on slavery in every state in America. The answer greatly angered the Southerners. In the end, following the debates, Stephen Douglas won the senatorial spot, but the Republicans -

although Lincoln lost - saw it as a "victory in defeat", giving their representative a much needed springboard for his following achievements.

Next up in the long list of Civil War causes was the all-important Presidential Election of 1860. When the overall American history is observed, we can see that no other election - before or since 1860 - has held so many consequences and dangers for a single nation. In 1860, there were several key candidates that ran for the position of the President of the United States. The great number of them was a direct result of the split between the pre-war parties, the collapse of the Whigs and the emergence of the Republicans. However, now it was all too likely that the Republicans had the winning candidate: Abraham Lincoln rose to great popularity in the anti-slavery North. For the Southerners, these were dire prospects. They knew all too well that almost the entirety of the North held abolitionist views. To that end, the idea of a Republican winner was a big threat for the South and its ideals. First and foremost, that would be a direct threat to the slavery on which South was established. But secondly, it also painted the whole of South as an "inferior" of the North. This was termed as "sectional inferiority", especially when the Republican intent of prohibiting slavery in all the territories was considered. As the tensions rose to threatening levels, an outpour of Southern protests emerged. Famously, the Mississippi Senator, Jefferson Davis, declared that the Souther submission to the Republican would be *intolerable to a proud people*. Everything seemed to be at stake now. The public attitude in the South boldly declared only one thing: if a Republican did become president, the South was ready and willing to consider seceding from the United States. This prospect made the presidential election of 1860 an dangerous "game" with incredibly high stakes.

Talk of secession in the South was becoming more and more frequent. Stephen Douglas attempted to no avail to divert the Southerners from this notion. He campaigned in the South, pleading for the Union, meeting animosity at every corner. A Memphis, Tennessee newspaper wrote famously about him:

"The bloated visage of Stephen A. Douglas is now turned toward the South. He commences his tramp to-day, and like an itinerant peddler of Yankee notions, will soon be hawking his pinchbeck principles over the South. He comes in our midst with no worthier motives than the incendiary."

"The War Approaching"
The Raid on Harpers Ferry

One of the tragic and scandalous events in those critical moments preceding the Civil War was the so-called "Harpers Ferry Raid". It was an unexpected - and somewhat foolish - event that only caused further instability between the North and the South. It was orchestrated by one John Brown, an abolitionist leader who rose to prominence as an active advocate for the Northern cause. However, he was well known (perhaps infamously) in Kansas as a strange and disturbed individual. He had strong religious convictions and believed himself to be an "instrument of God". Some, back in his home state, believed him to be thoroughly mad, which could be corroborated by the fact that there was a history of insanity in his family. But he was nonetheless well-liked. He was considered as a valuable proponent of the abolitionist cause, and a serious man with a strong moral compass. He was ambitious and charismatic, a fact that allowed him to win financial support across the North. In 1859, he was a man in his late fifties - but was still determined to contribute to the anti-slavery cause of the North. Because of this, he made a daring and controversial move: on the night of October 16th 1859, together with his three sons and 13 other individuals, he made a failed armed raid of the federal arsenal that was located at the town of Harper's Ferry in Virginia. With this raid, he attempted to seize a great quantity of weapons and ammo, flee to the inhospitable Appalachian mountains, and attempt to instigate a slave revolt in the South from there. However, his plan was full of flaws and inconsistencies, and was termed by many as downright suicidal. That it was.

At the start of the raid, everything went surprisingly smoothly. Brown and his raiding company captured the arsenal with ease, taking a few hostages along the way and inducing a couple of slaves to join in with him. But soon after, everything went wrong. The news of the raid spread, and the state militia detachments of both Virginia and Maryland states arrived at the scene, led by Colonel Robert E. Lee, a man who would rise to fame later on. Brown and his crew, now desperate, holed up in a fire engine house at the arsenal, where they were promptly surrounded. What ensued was a lengthy siege, lasting some 36 hours, where the militia troops made attempts to capture the raiders alive and make them surrender. But this was to no avail - Brown was zealously adamant about holding out. In the end, Robert E. Lee ordered his troops to storm the engine house. A brief exchange of fire ensued, with two of John Brown's sons dying before his eyes. Brown himself was captured alive, alongside six surviving members of his raiding party.

Soon after, Brown was tried for treason - but was adamant about standing by his cause. He refused an insanity plea, and claimed that he would die a "martyr's death". Until the end he spoke of helping the anti-slavery cause, but failed to realize that his actions contributed to a much greater disaster. He was tried, sentenced to death, and executed on December 2nd 1859. In his very last letter, he writes: *"I, John Brown, am now quite certain that the crimes of this guilty land will never be purged away but with Blood"*.

Still, his failed raid held great consequences. The entirety of the South was in shock after the event happened. In many ways, it was the unfolding of their biggest fears: abolitionists attempting to instigate a massive slave revolt. This wouldn't be all that serious if it weren't for the financial support that Brown had received from anonymous Northern backers. This meant that the bigger figures in the North shared his sentiment and sympathized with his actions at Harpers Ferry. But in truth, most big players in the North quickly condemned Brown's actions and distanced themselves from his cause. Many Republicans dubbed the raid as "fatally wrong" and "utterly repugnant". But the Southerners were not reassured. Newspapers in Richmond, Virginia, wrote: *"The Harpers Ferry invasion has advanced the cause of disunion more than any other event that has happened since the formation of its government".*

And that it was. The failed raid was, according to many leading historians, a "tragic prelude" and a dress rehearsal for the coming American Civil War.

History, however, was being made in 1860. As was expected, Abraham Lincoln, the Republican candidate, failed to make it onto the election ballots in ten of the Southern States. In fact, Lincoln did not win a single electoral vote from any of the 15 slave states. He was greatly despised there, before and after the war. But in the North, he was well-liked. In just a short amount of time, he re-entered politics and became known amongst the public, eventually becoming the leading Republican presidential candidate. Many say that he did things "by-the-book": he came from one of the key states, Illinois; in 1858 Congressional elections he managed to gain a nationwide reputation as a result of his skilled debates with Stephen Douglas; between 1859 and 1860, he made numerous speeches across the North, gaining supporters at every turn - all the while denying presidential ambitions; he skillfully avoided sticking to any ideologies and labels, thus appealing to a wide variety of voters; he lacked administrative experience, but shaped this into a reputation of honesty and integrity.

In the end, Abraham Lincoln took a sweeping victory in the North. He became the 16th President of the United States, and - to many - the greatest president in American history. Lincoln would be inaugurated in the following year, on March 4th, 1861. But while the abolitionist North rejoiced, the pro-slavery South talked about nothing else than - secession. This outcry was almost immediate, especially amongst the "fire eaters" - the party that wanted to leave the Union at once. It was considered that with Lincoln being in the White House, the South was in catastrophic peril.

Soon enough, a chain reaction occurred - with critical events developing at such a rapid pace as few could predict. The first to secede from the Union was South Carolina, well known as a hotspot of secessionist sentiments. It did so on December 20th 1860. By the following February, a number of states followed in its footsteps. In the so-called "Deep South", Georgia, Florida, Texas, and Alabama seceded as well. In many ways, the election of Lincoln caused a massive landslide in the South, leading to an inevitable conflict. The seceding states at once organized their own territories. They initially acted individually, but a sense of greater joint action in the whole of the South was unmistakable. On February 9th 1861, Mississippi's Jefferson Davis was elected by Southern delegates as the first provisional president of the *Confederate States of America*, and the capital of the latter was chosen - Montgomery in Alabama.

The stage for war was all set. The election of Abraham Lincoln was the final drop to overfill the cup. It was the "green light" that the South wanted, and the secession - peaceful up to that point - would soon boil over into an armed conflict, starting the American Civil War. On April 9th 1861, the Confederate (Southern) forces attacked the island fortress of Fort Sumter, in Charleston, South Carolina, thus starting four years of bloody civil war that pitted brother against brother, ripping the nation in two.

The War Begins

The American Civil War was a-brewing for a very long time. But the tumultuous brew finally reached the boiling point, and the road to open warfare was swift, brutal, and long-expected. The Southern states were quick to secede, forming the Confederate States of America. Initially, the Confederacy (better known as the "South") was comprised of the seven original slave states: Florida, Alabama, Mississippi, South Carolina, Georgia, Texas, and Lousiana. Soon after the war erupted, four additional slave-owning states joined the Confederacy: Tennessee, Virginia, Arkansas, and North Carolina. These were the states of the so-called "Upper South". Later in the war, Kentucky and Missouri were also accepted into the Confederacy.

Opposing them was the "North". This was formally known as the Union, or the United States of America with Abraham Lincoln at their helm. The stage was set for an obliterating, brotherly Civil War.

Just two months after the Confederate states have chosen their first (and only) president, Jefferson Davis, the war erupted with the southerners attacking Fort Sumter, in Charleston in South Carolina, on April 12th 1861. It was the first decisive "shot" of the war, a firm opening and a clear point of no return. But initially, both sides were reluctant to be the first to fire and drew the other into conflict. But there was a quite obvious point of contention, where conflict would undoubtedly break out. These were the Union-occupied forts in the Southern territories. Before secession, these were regular forts with a federal army garrison. But after secession, they were Union fortresses deep within the territory of the independent and sovereign Confederacy. Some of these forts were Charleston's Fort Moultrie, Fort Pickens in Pensacola Bay in Florida, and others. And one of the foremost of these fortresses was Fort Sumter, located in the middle of the harbor at Charleston, South Carolina. All of these defenses became the points of heated arguments between the two sides, almost immediately.

At Sumter, the young Major Robert Anderson based his troops. He recently moved them from the vulnerable Fort Moultrie to Fort Sumter, and there sat and waited. Determined to keep the fortresses in Federal hands, Abraham Lincoln instructed the Sumter garrison to wait and react only when and if fired upon. But in truth, his move from Moultrie to Sumter was unexpected and unauthorized, and seen by the South as an act of aggression. Most of the southerners expected Major Anderson to defect to their side and show his Confederate loyalties, him being a Kentucky native and all. But much to their surprise, Anderson followed his soldierly duty and remained loyal to the Union, staying firmly in Fort Sumter. Holed up in the fort, however, the major had enough supplies for just six weeks, which meant that reinforcements and resupply had to be provided at one point, threatening conflict. Another problem was the lack of troops at his disposal: Anderson commanded a small garrison of roughly 85 soldiers, while Fort Sumter required an imposing 650 men to be fully operational. Due to this, Anderson made the logical decision to operate only the lowest tier of the fortress, so as not to overstretch his troops.

Soon enough, it was becoming obvious that Fort Sumter would be a major point of contention. The North made attempts to reinforce the Southern-surrounded fort, in particular by an unarmed merchant vessel, the *"The Star of the West"*. However, as soon as the ship entered the waters on January 9th 1861, it was fired upon by Southern shore batteries, and driven off. Anderson refused to enter the fray, fearing that he might be the one to start an all-out war. In the meantime, the newly inaugurated Abraham Lincoln stated that the Union was determined to *"hold, occupy and possess the property and places belonging to the government"*. Tensions grew, but it was becoming apparent that Lincoln would have to reinforce Fort Sumter - one way or the other. To that end, the Union sent a new relief fleet towards Sumter, on

April 6th 1861. A lot was at stake, and many stated that America was "tip toeing on the edge of a knife". One wrong shot at Sumter would push the nation into a bloody Civil War. At the time, Senator Robert Toombs famously stated that *the firing on that fort will inaugurate a civil war greater than the world has yet seen*. Still, many southerners hoped that the situation would escalate into open violence, as that would draw the Upper South states to secede as well. Alas, many hands were forced at this time, as conflict could not be avoided. On one hand, the governor of South Carolina, Francis W. Pickens wanted to avoid drawing first blood at Sumter, however he was largely forced into action by the approaching Union resupply ship. To that end, the Confederate general P. G. T. Beauregard was ordered to request the fort's surrender. The time was now running out, and someone had to act. In the end, it would be Beauregard, the officer who is considered as starting the Civil War (which could not be averted by that point). Anderson still refused to give up the fort, knowing that reinforcements were on their way. Beauregard went into action. The Southerners gave Anderson a one hour forward notice, and then proceeded to bombard Fort Sumter, with the first shots fired around 4:30 am, April 12th. The cannonade was unleashed from the battery of "ironclads", with their 8 inch "columbiad" cannons, with the fiery shells announcing in their hellish thunder that the American Civil War had officially begun. History does not remember the first Southerner who fired those fated shots, but it does remember the Northerner who shot in response. It was the second in command of Major Anderson, one Captain Abner Doubleday. However, the garrison at Fort Sumter had no cannons equal to those of the Confederates, and their return fire was merely a show of defiance, and had no significant effects. Overall, the bombardment of Fort Sumter lasted 33 hours, and around 4,000 shells landed on the besieged garrison and the walls. Luckily, no soldiers died as the result of the battle, on either side. As for the result, the battle was a clear Confederate victory - Anderson stood no chance, especially being under-manned, without supplies, and running low on ammunition. At roughly 1.30 pm, on April 13th, he accepted the fate and surrendered. The news of the fall of Fort Sumter was received differently on either side. Undoubtedly, everyone knew that this began the civil war. On the Union side, a contemporary quote paints the dramatic situation at Sumter:

"By 11 a.m. the conflagration was terrible and disastrous. One-fifth of the fort was on fire, and the wind drove the smoke in dense masses into the angle where we had all taken refuge. It seemed impossible to escape suffocation. Some lay down close to the ground, with handkerchiefs over their mouths ... every one suffered severely ... the scene at this time was really terrific. The roaring and crackling of the flames, the dense masses of whirling smoke, the bursting of the enemy's shells, and our own which were exploding in the burning rooms, the crashing of the shot, and the sound of masonry falling in every direction, made the fort a pandemonium. When at last nothing was left of the building but the blackened walls and smoldering embers, it became painfully evident that an immense amount of damage had been done ... about 12:48 p.m. the end of the flag-staff was shot down, and the flag fell."

In the South, however, the news of the victory was received with zeal and passion, as the seceded states welcomed defiantly their stand against the North which they despised. The Governor of South Carolina, receiving news of the victory, famously stated to the gathered folk in front of the Charleston Hotel:

"Thank God! Thank God! The day has come; the war is open, and we will conquer or perish. We have defeated their twenty millions, and we have humbled the proud flag of the Stars and Stripes that never before lowered to any nation on earth. We have lowered it in humility before the Palmetto and Confederate flags, and have compelled them to raise a white flag and ask for honorable surrender. The Stars and Stripes have triumphed for 70 years, but on this 13th of April it has been humbled by the little State of South Carolina. And I pronounce here, before the

civilized world, that your independence is baptized in blood. Your independence is won upon a glorious battlefield, and you are free, now and forever, in defiance of the world in arms."

"History Made Through Warfare"
The First Battles of the American Civil War

The American Civil War is characterized with one peculiarity - it was a war of *many* battles. Many historians agree that there were in excess of 10,500 noticeable military engagements in the war - and listing even a part of them in this book would be an utterly impossible task. This count is narrowed down to roughly 50 *major* battles that have been studied in great detail, and around 100 smaller, but also significant engagements. And even with this narrowed count, we can understand that it is impossible to address every important and famous battle of the Civil War. To that end, we will touch upon only a few of the very famous and important battles.

At the onset of the Civil War, both North and South were confident in victory. The southerners hoped for a decisive and easy victory, while the northerners were confident that they could end the war with a single decisive strike. Some, however, thought that the situation would unfold somewhat differently. On the Northern side, the Union General-in-Chief, Winfield Scott, took a more logical and careful approach to planning the war. He knew that it would take several months to train and gather the needed amount of troops to defeat the Confederate states. To that end, he created and proposed the famed "Anaconda Plan", a strategy that aimed to suppress the Confederacy at the very start of the war. Scott understood the strategic importance of the Mississippi River, and devised a plan that was much alike an anaconda snake strangling its victim. The plan aimed to create a naval blockade of Southern ports, and to descend along the Mississippi River and cut the southern states in two. However, Abraham Lincoln wanted to land a quick and decisive blow on the Confederates, urging his general McDowell to march to Richmond, Virginia. On the other hand, Jefferson Davis, the President of the Confederacy, was determined to protect every part of his Confederate States, unwilling to lose even a part of them. What ensued would soon lay down the cards on the table. It was the first major battle of the American Civil War, the First Manassas, or the First Battle of Bull Run.

The state of Virginia was quickly becoming a major theater of war and the war's first battleground. In 1861, the Confederate general P. G. T. Beauregard, the so-called "Little Frenchman", was at the head of an army 22,000 strong, positioned to the south of the Bull Run river, at Manassas. The famed general Joe Johnston was positioned to the west of him, heading another army of 11,000 soldiers. Both armies were largely composed of inexperienced fresh troops. The Union forces knew of these Confederate encampments, and the Northern public urged them to attack. It was believed that one swift victory could bring a sudden end to the Confederacy. To that end, the Union dispatched General Irvin McDowell, who, yielding under political pressure, marched out on 16th July with some 30, 000 men at his disposal. These Union troops were equally inexperienced as their Southern counterparts. It soon came to blows, and the first major battle of the civil war was erupting. The Union army quickly took the upper hand, placing the Confederates at a big disadvantage. The Union attack of the 21st July was well conceived and well executed, placing the southern army under great pressure. Confederates - although composed of "green" troops - fought with bravery, especially the brigade of Brigadier General Thomas J. Jackson, which stood its ground no matter what. Following the battle, Thomas Jackson would become known as "Stonewall Jackson". And although the Union troops had the upper hand, things would soon change. General Johnston's troops traveled by train from Shenandoah, and reinforced the troops of Beauregard just in time. This was the tipping point that the Confederates needed. Flanked and outnumbered, the Union troops quickly panicked and turned into an all out disorganized run. The southerners claimed their first major victory in the war, and a great boost of morale. However, the battle left considerable casualties on both sides: the Confederacy had some 2,000 casualties, with 440 dead; and the Union had 3,000 casualties, with more than 600 dead.

With the victory secured, Beauregard and Johnston were positioned roughly some 30 miles from Washington DC, but even so they made no attempts to capitalize on their win and to march on the capital. Modern historians consider this as a failure, a missed chance to win the war with one bold stroke. However, chances of success were highly unlikely for the victorious Confederates - their troops were battered and bruised, inexperienced, in need of supplies and disorganized.

Following the First Manassas (First Battle of Bull Run), the Confederate morale was boosted, and their confidence solidified. The Union forces did not despair, however. Although they tasted defeat, they were still determined to continue the war effort and to avenge themselves on the southerners. However, in the following October, the Confederate army, commanded by Captain Nathan G. Evans, won a great victory at the Battle of Ball's Bluff. This further boosted Confederate spirits, and allowed their forces to maintain a defensive line along the Potomac River.

"A War of Firsts"
The Soldiers and the Battlefields in the American Civil War

When writing and discussing the American Civil War, it is very important to address the nature of warfare as it was back in those days. The 1860's and its technologies were at a true junction of the ages - not far enough to be modern for the time, and still not too outdated. In the decade following the Crimean War that abruptly swept through Eastern Europe, many new innovations in the field of warfare were beginning to be implemented by many nations across the world. Many of these changes were reflected - some for the first time - in the course of the Civil War. Consequently, many historians have called it the first true modern war. But in truth, the Civil War had modern elements mixed in with archaic ones. The grand strategy still relied on mass infantry charges and line battles, on cavalry and artillery, and sweeping flanking maneuvers. Still, even though warfare itself might have been outdated and costly in lives, it still benefited from some modern inventions that were pioneered in those years. Notable inventions included the telegraph, which allowed armies to communicate swiftly and over great distances. It provided a much needed and vital connection between the forces in the field, and the commanders in the background. Another benefit was the broad network of railroads that the United States boasted. Of course, this network was more common and widespread in the North, but it nevertheless provided a swift and efficient way for transportation of troops, reinforcements, and supplies - again, across great distances.

Weapons too saw modernization. Muskets were no longer of the old type. Now they received special rifling that would immensely change the nature of warfare. The rifling allowed soldiers to effectively engage targets at a much greater distance, with accuracy. The radical new invention was the Minié (Minie) ball, a hollow-based bullet that saw extensive use in the American Civil War. The bullet was capable of inflicting great damage, and - together with the rifling - did not lose accuracy at long ranges. Another key introduction to warfare was related to the navy: special Ironclad warships appeared, equipped with steam engines and heavy naval guns. They allowed greater strategic advantages and an upper hand in naval warfare. First rudimentary ambulances appeared as well, and first field hospitals. They opened up the way to more serious combat medicine that would become a major branch of the military in future conflicts. Lastly, the officers in the American Civil War were educated and capable, being schooled at the *United States Naval Academy at Annapolis* and the *United States Military Academy at West Point*.

But when we compare the armies of the South and the North, we can almost notice no differences whatsoever. After all, this was a single nation, a single people - split apart by the ravages of war. When the respective armies marched to war, they would fight in the same way, with the same weapons, and according to the same rules. Only the convictions were different, the backgrounds, the beliefs, and the traditions. In fact, the armies used the same instruction manuals. For example, one noted source tells us that both sides used *"Rifle and Light Infantry Tactics"*, written by Lieutenant Colonel William J. Hardee, as the chief instruction manual for their infantry troops. Of course, the common infantryman was by far the most versatile and most common troop type in the war. In the end, it was down to the common soldier to tip the scales of a battle, even if artillery and cavalry were regarded as the masters of war at the time.

Any changes between the two armies - aside their uniforms, markings, and insignia - would often appear from general to general, from brigade to brigade, and so on. But observing these battles, one could see little change: these were one people, in different uniforms. One quote says: *"these were two armies that were drawn from one nation*

– the men who faced each other at Bull Run, Gettysburg and Nashville, were more alike than not".

Of course, the opposing sides were all familiar with each other's weaponry, for it was for the most part - the same. In the later stages of the war, the Union forces did benefit from breech-loading rifles, but for the most part - the rifled muskets were the staple of both armies. In order to find weaknesses in their opponent's ranks, each army tried to develop new battleground tactics and new methods of warfare. Due to the increasing changes in warfare, the outdated "packed rank" advance was quickly growing obsolete: thick lines of soldiers marching steadily across the field was a near-suicidal tactic that caused mass casualties on either side. A new and unique tactic, known as "advance by rush", was preferred instead, but costly as well - any direct assault against prepared defences or entrechments was nearly suicidal. A notable episode from the Civil War that gives us a great insight into the devastation of mass charges happened in November of 1864, during the Battle of Franklin, when the General of the Confederate army, John Bell Hood, ordered a direct charge against prepared Union positions, and lost around 7,000 men in a short amount of time.

Still, the officers played an immensely important role in the American Civil War. The performance of hte officer corps was instrumental for the course of the war as we know it today. Interesting to note is the fact that the Confederacy had a distinct advantage in this matter: at the outbreak of the civil war, the majority of military academies - some seven or eight of them - were located within the Southern states. But where the Confederacy could boast a capable officer corps, the Union could counter with significantly better logistics, railway networks, resources, and materiel. Furthermore, the North could benefit from a well-developed recruitment network, with great numbers of volunteers joining the ranks initially, and during the war. In fact, in the very opening stages of the war, Abraham Lincoln saw his rank swell with 75,000 fresh volunteer troops. The Union's number of troops was increasing throughout the war, and other advantages also kept increasing. Lincoln famously stated in 1864, as the war was nearing its end: *"We have more men now than we had when the war began. We are gaining strength and may, if need be, maintain the contest indefinitely."*

But ultimately, we cannot avoid the fact that the American Civil War - and its many battlefields - was a brutal, vicious, bloody, and controversial conflict. For the first time, many radical and questionable war practices began to appear, and the world could only watch in mute horror. For example, with the slavery being the focal point of the war, racial discrimination ran rampant amongst the troops - especially in the South. Massacres were not uncommon, sadly. One notable event is related to the Confederate General Nathan Bedoford Forrest, who was involved in a massacre during the Battle of Fort Pillow. There, the troops under his command massacred hundreds of surrendered Union soldiers, most of them black. This event - and others like it - are a great stain on the history of the United States, and one of the dark aspects of the American Civil War. Other uncommon methods of warfare were also practiced. For example, during the Siege of Petersburg, Union army engineers dug a tunnel beneath the Confederate positions, storing explosives for weeks. Then, just before their attack, they detonated their charges beneath the unexpecting Confederate soldiers, creating a devastating, enormous explosion of a magnitude never before seen. The amount of stored gunpowder was roughly 8,000 lbs (3,600 kilograms), which gives us a perfect insight into the magnitude of the explosion and the size of the engineering work.

Another popular and (for the time) innovative method of warfare was the early form of the sniper. The so-called "sharpshooters" were present on both sides in the Civil War, and posed a real hidden threat for the common soldiers. These soldiers were well-equipped, highly trained, and deadly at long distances.

But for the common infantryman, war was always hell. Marching steadily in close, tightly packed ranks, closing in on the enemy lines that are ready to fire - was nothing short of vicious and horrific combat. Burdened by the dated nature of the musket rifle, the Civil War's common soldier was ever at peril. Theirs was the ultimate sacrifice, and their memory needs to be always preserved.

"Fates Decided"
The War Continues

Following the first major battle of the American Civil War, the First Manassas, the world watched in disbelief. America - that nation that fought so hard to gain its independence - was now descended into a bitter and vicious conflict. This first battle was a major wake up call for all the politicians and war-mongers across America and in Europe. Because the First Manassas was no mere clash - it was a devastating battle that left hundreds of young men dead and many more viciously maimed. Judging by that first battle, the war would not be over swiftly as many had hoped. The "rebellion" of the southern states, as the Union termed it, would not be crushed quickly and with one swift stroke. The American Civil War was starting in earnest, and it promised to be a brutal and unforgiving war of brothers in feud.

Receiving a chilly wake up call at First Manassas, the Northerners had to once again sit down behind the strategist's table. Their command needed a new solution on ending the war quickly. Several plans were put forward, with the most attention given to the elaborate plan of the aged General Scott - known as the "Anaconda" plan. His ideas were first presented to Abraham Lincoln on May 2nd 1861. Scott envisioned a vast blockade of the south, employing a *"cordon of posts on the Mississippi to its mouth from the junction with the Ohio River, and by blockading ships of war on the seaboard"*. Like a giant anaconda snake, this blockade was meant to "strangle" the South, until it had to surrender. However, the majority of the Union leaders saw this plan as slow and inefficient: most of them wanted a swift and decisive course of action. Scott himself - an elderly veteran - was aware of this, and commented that the *greatest obstacle in the way of this plan – the great danger now pressing upon us – is the impatience of our patriotic and loyal Union friends"*. He said that there were constant demands for *"instant and vigorous action, regardless of consequences".* After much deliberation, Scott's blockade was put into action. It would go on to require active monitoring of roughly 3,500 miles (5,600 km) of coastlines, greatly hampering Confederate harbors and supply lines. The blockade lasted throughout the war, and in the end it proved to be a powerful and effective "weapon" for the Union, as it caused a severe economic impact on the Southern states. Officially declaring the blockade as active, Abraham Lincoln made his historic speech to the citizens of the Union:

"Whereas an insurrection against the Government of the United States has broken out in the States of South Carolina, Georgia, Alabama, Florida, Mississippi, Louisiana, and Texas, and the laws of the United States for the collection of the revenue cannot be effectually executed therein conformably to that provision of the Constitution which requires duties to be uniform throughout the United States: And whereas a combination of persons engaged in such insurrection, have threatened to grant pretended letters of marque to authorize the bearers thereof to commit assaults on the lives, vessels, and property of good citizens of the country lawfully engaged in commerce on the high seas, and in waters of the United States: And whereas an Executive Proclamation has been already issued, requiring the persons engaged in these disorderly proceedings to desist therefrom, calling out a militia force for the purpose of repressing the same, and convening Congress in extraordinary session, to deliberate and determine thereon: Now, therefore, I, Abraham Lincoln, President of the United States, with a view to the same purposes before mentioned, and to the protection of the public peace, and the lives and property of quiet and orderly citizens pursuing their lawful occupations, until Congress shall have assembled and deliberated on the said unlawful proceedings, or until the same shall ceased, have further deemed it advisable to set on foot a blockade of the ports within the States aforesaid, in pursuance of the laws of the United States, and of the law of Nations, in such case provided. For this purpose a competent force will be

posted so as to prevent entrance and exit of vessels from the ports aforesaid. If, therefore, with a view to violate such blockade, a vessel shall approach, or shall attempt to leave either of the said ports, she will be duly warned by the Commander of one of the blockading vessels, who will endorse on her register the fact and date of such warning, and if the same vessel shall again attempt to enter or leave the blockaded port, she will be captured and sent to the nearest convenient port, for such proceedings against her and her cargo as prize, as may be deemed advisable. And I hereby proclaim and declare that if any person, under the pretended authority of the said States, or under any other pretense, shall molest a vessel of the United States, or the persons or cargo on board of her, such person will be held amenable to the laws of the United States for the prevention and punishment of piracy. In witness whereof, I have hereunto set my hand, and caused the seal of the United States to be affixed. Done at the City of Washington, this nineteenth day of April, in the year of our Lord one thousand eight hundred and sixty-one, and of the Independence of the United States the eighty-fifth."

The War Years

Following the first engagements and the first major steps of the war, both sides worked busily on mobilization of troops. This was a game of numbers - as most wars are - and both sides knew it very well. Abraham Lincoln conducted a ferocious recruitment campaign, especially after that first surprising defeat at First Manassas. At once he signed a document, inviting well over 500,000 volunteers into the Union army, with a three year contract. By 1862, the Union had well over 700,000 volunteers, and the Confederacy over 500,000. Union recruits began amassing at military camps near Washington, and the Northerners were ready for new campaigning. General McDowell, who lost the battle at First Manassas, was promptly replaced by a slightly more seasoned General George McClellan, who would soon after become the General-in-Chief of the Union Army. McClellan organized the troops and created a powerful army, which he dubbed the Army of the Potomac. This army was one of the principal forces of the Union, helping it in the long run, even though McClellan did not run it to the best of his abilities. This was because he was somewhat indecisive in his early actions. In fact, in 1862 he was commanding a sizable force: some 120,000 infantry, 15,000 cavalry, 44 artillery pieces, and 1,100 transport wagons. However, he delayed with his initial plan of marching on the Confederate capital, Richmond, thinking that his opponent was numerically superior - even though he was not. This indecisiveness lasted for the good part of spring in 1862, and when McClellan at last decided to march, he was met in the field by a Southern army led by General Joseph Johnston. What ensued was a vicious two-day clash, known as the Battle of Seven Pines. This battle was led from May 31st to June 1st, 1862, and saw the Confederate General, the seasoned Joseph Johnston, attempting to defeat two Union Corps that were located at an isolated spot south of the Chickahominy River. The battle was one of the fiercest in the war:

several waves of southern attacks - somewhat disoriented - drove back the IVth Corps of the Union army. Throughout the clash, both sides received numerous reinforcements, which only led to high casualties. However, the Union army at last managed to stabilize their positions - thanks to reinforcements from the IInd and IIIrd Corps - but neither side had the advantage. In the end, the battle ended as inconclusive. However, both sides claimed to have won - even though no accomplishment was achieved. Nevertheless, the Battle of Seven Pines was important in many ways. It led directly to the appointment of the legendary Robert E. Lee to the Confederate command, since Joseph Johnston was seriously wounded during the battle. Lee's later campaigns would contribute greatly to the Confederate cause. Furthermore, the Battle of Seven Pines was the largest battle fought in the Eastern Theater of the American Civil War up to that time, and was second only to Shiloh - in terms of casualties. It was a costly battle on both sides, with roughly 6,000 casualties on the Confederate side (of which 980 men were killed), and some 5,000 casualties on the Union side (of which 790 men were killed). Last, but not least, the Battle of the Seven Pines marked the closest Union forces came to the Confederate capital of Richmond in their offensive.

With Joseph Johnston seriously wounded, the enthusiastic General Robert E. Lee took over the command that same evening. This was his time to shine and to display his skills as a military commander. From the get-go, he was bent on taking the initiative and to change his tactics from defensive to offensive. He renamed the Confederate army as "Army of Northern Virginia", and planned to join up his forces with General Jackson (Stonewall Jackson) and proceed to flank the Union troops. Robert E. Lee knew quite well that he could not wage war purely on the defensive, risking his armies to be "picked off" by the Union at will. To that end, he employed a unique "offensive-defensive" strategy, which was quite efficient when observed today, but at the time was somewhat criticized. Lee went on the offensive, hoping to score a major decisive victory that would undermine the Union morale. Lee began this plan near the end of June 1862, starting a week of battle operations that would come to be known as "The Seven Days", or the Seven Days Battles. Almost at the start, Union General McClellan lost the initiative, allowing Lee to seize the chance and begin a series of attacks - first at the battle of Mechanicsville (Beaver Dam Creek) on June 26th, then at the Battle of Gaines's Mill on June 27th, and then at the Battle of Savage's Station on June 29th. However, Lee lost the chance to catch the retreating Union army, and they managed to take up defensive positions on a strongly fortified hill. This resulted in the Battle of Malvern Hill, where Confederate forces assaulted strong Union positions and suffered immense casualties - some 5000 men compared to 3000 on the Union side.

In total, the Seven Days campaign was a costly one - the Confederacy lost some 20,600 men, while the Union losses were only 15,849. The main aspects of the poor Confederate performance were the delays in high command, with Stonewall Jackson losing several chances due to slow movements. Still, the campaign was a strategic success for the Confederates: Robert E. Lee managed to save the capital of Richmond, and to send McClellan retreating inland. The Seven Days campaign was subject to much study by military historians, and Robert E. Lee is generally praised for his initiative and his skill as a commander. James McPherson writes:

"... the Confederacy had a chance to win the war – not by conquering the North or destroying its armies, but by sapping the Northern will and capacity to conquer the South and destroy Confederate armies. On three occasions the Confederacy came close to winning on these terms. Each time it was Lee who almost pulled it off. His victories at the Seven Days and second Manassas battles and the invasion of Maryland in the summer of 1862; his triumph at Chancellorsville and the invasion of Pennsylvania in 1863; and the casualties his army inflicted on Grant's forces in the Wilderness–Petersburg campaign in the spring and summer

of 1864 ... these three campaigns each came close to sapping the Northern will to continue the war .... Of all Confederate commanders, Lee was the only one whose victories had some potential for winning the war. The notion that a more gradual strategy would have done better is speculative at best."

Soon after the Seven Days' battles were over, another crucial clash of the American Civil War ensued: **the Second Battle of Bull Run (Second Manassas)**. Before it, Lincoln had no intent on abandoning the idea of capturing Richmond. He ordered his General Pope to take command of the Union forces near Washington, while McClellan was ordered to join his forces with Pope. Together, they were to advance to Richmond. However, Robert E. Lee was determined to seize initiative - even though he suffered great casualties at Malvern Hill. He marched northwards in August, leading an army of some 55,000 men. These forces were split in half: one part was commanded by Lee's "right hand man", Stonewall Jackson. Jackson was instructed to make a long flanking sweep to the west and north of General Pope's forces - which were still awaiting the arrival of McClellan's troops. Stonewall Jackson achieved success, capturing Pope's main supply depot which was situated at Manassas. But in the meantime, McClellan's troops joined Pope, and the latter chose to eagerly descend upon the outnumbered army of Stonewall Jackson. But what the Northerners did not know was the fact that Robert E. Lee, with his 25,000 men, was marching to Stonewall's aid. The resulting clash was a total Union disaster: the Confederates attacked their left flank, sending their army into a panicked retreat. Still, Lee failed to achieve that decisive victory he wanted, since the majority of Union troops retreated in time. On the Union side, Lincoln quickly became aware that appointing the inexperienced Pope was a mistake - his poor leadership proved costly for the Northerners, as they lost some 16,000 men - compared to just 9,000 on the Confederate side. Due to this, Lincoln was quick to reinstate McClellan as the commander-in-chief of the Union forces.

The Battle of Antietam

While the Union morale was somewhat shaken, the Confederate commander Robert E. Lee was bolstered by his war victories. He did not want to waste time, and thus quickly continued his northern campaign. In September, he dispatched Stonewall Jackson to capture the garrison at Harper's Ferry, while he intended to lead an army 40,000 strong and invade Maryland. His plans with this invasion were to secure Maryland volunteers, to score that decisive major victory he wanted, to gain British recognition of the Confederate States, to demoralize the North even further, and to ultimately protect Virginia and its harvest. However, as soon as he dispatched Stonewall, two Union soldiers managed to gain the copies of his plans by sheer luck, providing the information to the Union command. At once, McClellan decided to use this newly created situation and moved to attack one part of the Confederate forces - i.e. Robert E. Lee. However, another turn of events meddled with his plans: a local Confederate sympathizer informed Lee of the threat. The latter at once reacted, and the Southern forces were forced to abandon the plan of invasion, and instead began gathering close to the village of Sharpsburg. Defensive positions were assembled around the village and at the western side of Antietam Creek, a tributary of the Potomac River.

As we can see, the situation was far from ideal for both parties involved. Before things went awry, Robert E. Lee *"had the most brilliant prospects that the Confederates ever had"*. But that would be the reality if things were simply ideal. They, however, were not. Straggling and desertion were rampant in the Confederate army, and Lee lost more soldiers than he hoped to gain in Maryland. To make matters worse, the lost battle plans that ended in Union hands only further deteriorated his situation. Because of all of this, Lee was forced to retreat back. But curiously enough, Lee did not fall back into Virginia, but took positions at Antietam, even though he was potentially outnumbered, flanked, and inhibited by the Potomac River behind him. For the Confederates, a lot was at stake here. If the Union commander McClellan was to react early on, while Lee's army was still split, his victory would be almost certain. However, he delayed again. In the meantime, Stonewall Jackson's detached army rejoined the main forces of Lee, helping to reduce the odds against the Confederates. Nevertheless, the Northerners had more men at their disposal. The stage was now set for what was to become one of the bloodiest battles in American history. The Battle of Antietam, fought on September 17th, was one of the darkest pages of the American Civil War, and was an immensely costly and vicious clash, with the highest number of casualties.

Beginning with a powerful flanking attack on the Confederate defenses, Antietam was a costly battle that was composed of a series of disjointed assaults. The Confederate forces hung on desperately, fending off attacks one after the other. However, many military historians criticize McClellan for his ineffectiveness, as his assaults were successfully - but not exploited and followed through. Due to this, Robert E. Lee managed to hold on. At a crucial point during the battle, Union forces led by General Burnside made great success, capturing the stone bridge over Antietam, threatening the Confederate right Flank. However, just when things seemed dire, the legendary Confederate General, A. P. Hill, showed up with his forces and launched a surprising counterattack on the Union positions, ultimately saving Robert E. Lee's right flank and collapsing the flank of Burnside. In the end, the battle ended as indecisive. However, the Union side was able to claim victory, because Robert E. Lee ultimately retreated back into Virginia. Still, the battle could have ended differently, and the Confederate forces could have been utterly crushed and defeated - but McClellan was once more indecisive, passive, and frightened. In the battle's decisive moments, when Burnside requested more men and cannons, McClellan failed to provide them, even though he had two fresh Corps of infantry at his disposal. He was frightened to use them, and thus remained passive throughout. All of his indecision gave Lee time to act, and for A. P. Hill to deliver his forces from Harper's Ferry in time to relieve him. Furthermore, when the battle was over and the Confederates began retreating back into Virginia, McClellan failed to pursue them and capitalize on the outcome. This greatly angered Abraham Lincoln. Due to this, near the end of the year, Lincoln once again dismisses McClellan, and places Ambrose Burnside in his place. Lincoln demanded from his new commander-in-chief to at once create a new campaign aimed at Richmond, Virginia. Burnside proposed that an army of 130,000 men be led towards Fredericksburg, south of the Confederate capital.

The Battle of Antietam remains one of the most tragic days in American history. It was the bloodiest one-day battle of the entire American Civil War. The Confederates lost a bit over 10,000 men (of which 1,500 were killed), and the Union lost more than 12,000 men (of which 2,100 were killed). Some sources claim that the number of killed men is even higher - with roughly 7,650 men dying that day. Nevertheless, the casualties were immense. The world watched in horror as the events unfolded in America. Furthermore, more Americans died in the Battle of Antietam than on any other day in the history of this nation. For that reason, it is well known as the "bloodiest day in American history".

"No other campaign and battle in the war had such momentous, multiple consequences as Antietam. In July 1863 the dual Union triumphs at Gettysburg and Vicksburg struck another blow that blunted a renewed Confederate offensive in the East and cut off the western third of the Confederacy from the rest. In September 1864 Sherman's capture of Atlanta electrified the North and set the stage for the final drive to Union victory. These also were pivotal moments. But they would never have happened if the triple Confederate offensives in Mississippi, Kentucky, and most of all Maryland had not been defeated in the fall of 1862."

Almost at once after the Battle of Antietam, Abraham Lincoln issued his famous Proclamation of Emancipation, on September 22nd, 1862. The document was both a presidential proclamation and an executive order, and was meant to proclaim the freedom of all enslaved people in the ten states in rebellion. This of course, was directed at the Confederate States. An African-American slave would, once free from Confederate governement (by runnign away to the Union side), become a free citizen. The famous proclamation read:

"That on the first day of January in the year of our Lord, one thousand eight hundred and sixty-three, all persons held as slaves within any State, or designated part of a State, the people whereof shall then be in rebellion against the United States shall be then, thenceforward, and forever free;

and the executive government of the United States, including the military and naval authority thereof, will recognize and maintain the freedom of such persons, and will do no act or acts to repress such persons, or any of them, in any efforts they may make for their actual freedom."

The Battle of Fredericksburg

Antietam proved to be a major turning point of the war. Robert E. Lee lost his initiative, and was forced to retreat back into Virginia. Still, he did so not overly battered - the general incompetence of the Union high command was highly criticized by Abraham Lincoln. After Antietam, Lincoln was adamant about pursuing the Confederate army into Virginia, keeping up the pressure that he hoped would break the enemy forces. Oddly enough, Robert E. Lee - with his unshakable spirits and enthusiasm - was also inclined to keep up the offensive, perhaps still hoping for that decisive victory to tip the scales. However, his army was not in the ideal shape for this, so he had to strike camp, rest, refit, and resupply. On his tail was the Union Army of the Potomac, still headed by General McClellan, who was already at fault with Lincoln. The latter ordered him to act, and McClellan finally began transferring his army across the Potomac River. However, he did so in his own fashion - slowly, hesitantly, fearfully, and highly lethargic. Abraham Lincoln had enough of this incompetence and lack of initiative and offensive spirit, so he replaced McClellan on November 7th, placing Major General Ambrose Burnside on his place. Burnside at last did as Lincoln wished, so he prepared a hasty offensive against the Confederates, with the aim of seizing Richmond. His plan was somewhat simple: lead 100,000 men into Virginia, cross the Rappahannock River swiftly and surprise the Confederates at Fredericksburg, win the city - and then continue south towards Richmond, racing before Lee's army could stop him. Simple and possibly efficient. Lincoln approved of the plan, and Burnside began his maneuvers, crossing the Rappahannock River. His move was swift and well executed. By November 15th, the Army of the Potomac, split into three "Grand Divisions", numbering some 120,000 troops, began its march and caught the Confederate troops by surprise. What ensued was the bloody Battle of Fredericksburg.

The city of Fredericksburg, however, was guarded by a natural obstacle - the river. It was the topmost priority for Burnside to cross this wide water, and it was a high urgency to build adequate pontoons. However, there was a considerable delay in delivery of pontoons due to bureaucratic difficulties, and this delay gave Robert E. Lee plenty of time to react, assemble his troops and prepare defenses. By the time the pontoon bridges were finally delivered, two corps of Lee's forces were already in their positions, facing the Union troops. Still, it had to be noted that Burnside didn't idly wait - he too prepared his troops and positions. But the Confederates had the clear upper hand. They placed their troops in strategic defensive positions, with Longstreet's Corps positioned at Marye's Heights behind the town, with a great concentration of troops and artillery emplacements. To his right were the Corps of Stonewall Jackson, equally well spread out. This meant that Burnside's troops looked at an immense defensive wall, with well over 70,000 men stretched across 13 kilometers (8 miles). Every one of these men was ready for defense and had a clear view of the valley below. Attacking these positions was equal to suicide - and that is exactly what Burnside did. He felt he was too invested, too committed to the operation and unable to abandon it. And so, on December 11th, he began crossing the river.

The crossing was a mess from the start. Constant harassing fire from Confederate sharpshooters, especially those of the Mississippi Brigade, made the setup of the pontoons a true nightmare. The city's buildings were deserted by the populace, and they gave excellent cover and vantage points to the sharpshooters. Union artillery attempted to drive them off, and thus reduced much of the city to rubble. The harrassors were only driven out when the Union troops at last crossed the river. By December 12th, most of the Union troops marched across the pontoon bridging, entering the deserted Fredericksburg. The next day, it came to blows. The Confederates were simply too well entrenched to be budged out of place. Each assault that the Union troops conducted was repulsed - with heavy losses. The suffering was especially prevalent at the so-called "Marye's Heights" above the town, where General Longstreet's troops were placed. Here, several Union brigades were almost mindlessly sent to their doom, assaulting well placed positions only to be repulsed time and time again. These assaults had to be conducted *uphill*, across *open ground*, and in direct *line of artillery fire*. It was true slaughter. As one witness of the battle told Abraham Lincoln: *it was slaughter.* The worst killing ground was at the so-called "sunken road", where some 2,000 Confederate troops were positioned behind a wall and backed by a hill swarming with Confederate troops. The Union soldiers attacking this point were continuously moved down by the southern infantry that kept up a rapid pace of fire. The Battle of Fredericksburg was an incredible slaughter, a great loss of human life. By the end, Ambrose Burnside lost some 12,700 men (of which some 1,200 were killed) - needlessly. On the other hand, the Confederates lost just 5,400 (of which 608 were killed). By December 15th, the battle was done, and Burnside withdrew back across the river. Fredericksburg was a decisive and strong Confederate victory.

The slaughterhouse that this battle was, seriously shook Northern morale and was highly criticized in Washington D.C. On the other hand, Southerners rejoiced about their victory. Lincoln was targeted too, as a result. He was highly criticized, and an anti-war sentiment began spreading amongst Union troops.

What is more, Ambrose Burnside's reputation was at stake too. Receiving command, he did not prove himself. Instead, he led his troops to certain doom. He hoped to salvage his stained reputation with another attempted crossing of the Rappahannock, trying to outflank Robert E. Lee. His second try was an utter failure, due to the impassable muddy roads that prevented rapid movement. This was soon called off, leaving Burnside's reputation stained. He was promptly relieved of the high command, and replaced with Major General Joe Hooker, noted for his aggressive and fighting spirit.

Roughly in the middle of 1863, there was a major turning point in the war. Several key battles definitely left their marks on both warring parties. However, the North could more easily and quickly replace and replenish the lost forces and supplies, mostly thanks to their logistics and a major volunteer force. In May of that year, Robert E. Lee met with Jefferson Davis in Richmond, Virginia, in order to discuss the current state of the war and the future plans of the Confederacy. The ambitious and enthusiastic Northern General, Ulysses Grant, was giving them major troubles on the Western Front of the war, and Lee, encouraged by his fantastic victories at both Fredericksburg (December 1862) and Chancellorsville (April 1863), wanted to achieve another victory in Union territories. Thus, it was decided to once again march into the North and invade it, but this time in Pennsylvania. This new campaign saw Lee marching north and dividing the Southern army into three parts. However, he did not know the exact location of the Union Army. On July 1st, however, several Southerner detachments chanced upon the already encamped Northerners in Gettysburg. Robert E. Lee did not hesitate: he launched an ambitious attack on July 1st, leaving the bulk of his army in the background - since the Union forces were not in full force either. The Union forces, however, had excellent and advantageous defensive positions on the hilly ground, which Lee intended to take by force. He failed to do so due to a misunderstanding in communication with his officers, and in the meantime northern reinforcements arrived. As the battle unfolded, Lee had to make a number of tactical decisions, and was further hampered with arguing and disagreements with General James Longstreet. In fact, it was Longstreet who pointed out that the assault on the ridge positions would ultimately prove to be futile. His words to Robert E. Lee are often quoted as such:

"I've been a soldier all my life. I've fought from the ranks on up, you know my service. But sir, I must tell you now, I believe this attack will fail. No 15,000 men ever made could take that ridge. It's a distance of more than a mile, over open ground. When the men come out of the trees, they will be under fire from Yankee artillery from all over the field. And those are Hancock's boys! And now, they have the stone wall like we did at Fredericksburg."

Furthermore, Lee received misinformation from his spies. He finally made the decision to stay put and continue the fight. Thus unfolded the Battle of Gettysburg, one of the bloodiest fights of the American Civil War, and also one of its major turning points. On the battle's first day, Confederate forces managed to break through the hastily assembled Union troops, sending them into a run. However, the battle was still not concluded. On the second day, both the armies were in full count and assembled, and the battle raged on in earnest. The Confederates launched fierce attacks along the battle line, especially towards the Union left flank. Still, against all odds, the Union lines held out and did not fold - despite suffering immense losses. And thus, the battle raged on into its third day. This third day - the culmination of the clash - was marked by an iconic event that would live on in history. It was known as the "Pickett's Charge" - a desperate assault where some 12,500 Confederate soldiers made a futile charge against Union positions. The attack was aimed at the very center of Union positions at the location known as Cemetery Ridge. With concentrated artillery and rifle fire, the Union troops quickly repelled this charge and caused major casualties for the Confederates. Many termed it as a major mistake, a battlefield error from which the South would never recover, militarily and psychologically. Either way, the battle ended soon after this failed charge. It was a battle of immense casualties: the Union side had around 23,000 casualties (of which 3,150 were killed), while the Confederacy had up to 28,000 casualties (of which up to 5,000 were killed). Gettysburg ended as a strong Union victory, which helped solidify the reputation of General George G. Meade as a seasoned and competent leader. Lee, however, was listing his initiative. One quote sums it up thus:

"The results of this victory are priceless. [...] The charm of Robert E. Lee's invincibility is broken. The Army of the Potomac has at last found a general that can handle it, and has stood nobly up to its terrible work in spite of its long disheartening list of hard-fought failures. [...] Copperheads are palsied and dumb for the moment at least. [...] Government is strengthened four-fold at home and abroad."

Hoping to gain that crucial victory to tip the scales of the war, Robert E. Lee took one risk too many. This defeat was an immense setback for the Confederacy, and in many ways led to their ultimate defeat in the American Civil War. Following the defeat, Robert E. Lee led his battered army into a tormenting retreat back into Virginia. Meade's Army of the Potomac followed in pursuit, and a string of minor battles and clashes ensued. In the end, Lee made a hasty crossing of the Potomac, finally retreating and bringing an end to his disastrous Gettysburg Campaign in July 1863. Bruce Catton, in his monumental work, "Glory Road", comments on the battle's aftereffects:

"[The Army of the Potomac] had won a victory. It might be less of a victory than Mr. Lincoln had hoped for, but it was nevertheless a victory—and, because of that, it was no longer possible for the Confederacy to win the war. The North might still lose it, to be sure, if the soldiers or the people should lose heart, but outright defeat was no longer in the cards."

Still, even though Robert E. Lee's reputation for invincibility was seriously shaken, and Union morale was at its highest; the Gettysburg disaster was not the fend for the Confederacy. This was mostly because General Meade was unable to fully follow through with his victory and exploit it.

The Union continued their victorious streak and gained some extremely important victories during 1863 - but not in Virginia. Apart from the Battles of Vicksburg and Gettysburg, they achieved another victory at Chattanooga in November 1863, where General Ulysses Grant proved to be the best general of the Union. Southern morale was slowly falling, but Lee and his troops were still present in the east and posed a formidable threat nonetheless. The following year was an election year, and there was hope that a candidate ready to make peace would be chosen. Grant's successes earned him the title of first commander of the Western forces and then of the entire army of the Union. He immediately focused on the east, in order to better "supervise" Lee's Confederate army. Together with General Sherman, he discussed the Union's next crucial move. He didn't want to complicate things further, for he ultimately knew that they were numerically stronger and better supplied than the Southerners. He felt it was best for both sides to end the war as quickly as was possible, and to that end he planned to attack as much and as strongly as was possible. In just two weeks, a viable written plan was arranged. The armies scattered throughout the territory would simultaneously launch their campaigns and move toward the same goal. Ulysses Grant would march with his 115,000 men to face Robert E. Lee in Virginia, and General Sherman would conquer Atlanta and infiltrate the heart of the Confederacy, inflicting all sorts of possible damage. These were the two main campaigns, and there were a few smaller ones besides them, but they served as general support. On the other hand, Southerners found it difficult to gather new recruits. They moved the upper and lower age limits for access to the army, and those soldiers whose contract expired were forced to remain in service. This meant that it was often the case that boys were caught up in the whirlwinds of war, left to do a man's job at a young age. And still, despite these measures, the whole Confederate military strength was less than half of what the northerners had at their disposal. To that end, the southern commander, Robert E. Lee, chose to play defense on his home soil of Virginia.

"A Major Turning Point"
The Union's offensive

It was now becoming clear that the Union was gaining an upper hand in the war, and that the drawing curtains were slowly beginning to fall. A major Union offensive began in the spring of 1864, and the northerners descended upon the South in one fell swoop. With his campaign, General Grant - now the foremost commander of the Union - wanted to instigate Robert E. Lee to defend Richmond. However, throughout the Union's campaign, Lee skillfully anticipated all of Grant's moves, and withdrew accordingly as they progressed. After the army crossed the Rapidan River, they clashed with Southerners in the counties of Spotsylvania and Orange. The terrain was inaccessible, wooded and full of thickets. Grant wanted to get out of this terrain as quickly as possible, but Lee, as soon as he learned of his plans, attacked him in the wild, which resulted in a fierce battle that was accordingly named - the Battle of the Wilderness. It was fought from May 5th to 7th, 1864 in a heavily wooded area close to Fredericksburg. After two days of intense fighting, both sides suffered high casualties - some 29,000 in total. It was another terrifying episode of the American Civil War, and one of its costliest battles. Yet even so, the result was inconclusive - as Grant eventually disengaged his armies and continued his offensive, while the Southerners withdrew. In many ways, the disengagement was Grant's attempt to lure Robert E. Lee into another battle, under more favorable conditions for the Union troops. To that end, the northerners moved on to the district of Spotsylvania under Grant's orders. What ensued was the crucial Battle of Spotsylvania Court House, fought from May 9th to May 21st, 1864. Before the battle began, Lee managed to reach the crucial Spotsylvania positions before Grant, and there began entrenching his troops in formidable defensive positions. The result was a vicious trench battle with occasional assaults, as Grant tried various things in order to break the Confederate positions. This was the bloodiest battle of Grant's campaign. Both sides again lost thousands of casualties, in a never before seen episode of the war. In total, over 32,000 casualties were present on both sides. However, the battle was again inconclusive. Still, both sides claimed victory at Spotsylvania: the Union because they continued their offensive while inflicting immense losses to the enemy, and the Confederacy because they held their positions.

Grant then moved further south toward Richmond, and Lee followed in his footsteps. The two armies clashed a few more times in minor battles, such as the North Anna River battle or the clash at Totopotomoy Creek. Still, these were just minor skirmishes. In late May and the next ten days, one of the bloodiest battles in American history took place, the Battle of Cold Harbor. After the series of clashes at the North Anna River, Grant once again disengaged and swung around to the Southeast, around Lee's right flank. He then seized the crossroads at Cold Harbor, just 10 miles from Richmong, Virginia, the capital of the Confederacy. The southerners arrived and dug themselves into elaborate trenches and earthworks, with the northerners unsuccessfully attempting to breach these positions by frontal attacks. The Battle of Cold Harbor was fought from May 31st to June 12th 1864, and can be seen as the bloodiest, most destructive battle of the entire American Civil War. It was a catastrophic clash of the two armies, and resulted in immense loss of life. Most of the casualties were on the Union side, as their soldiers came in wave after wave onto the Confederate earthworks, only to be repeatedly repelled and killed en-masse. After the war, General Grant expressed regret for the futile assaults at Cold Harbor: *I have always regretted that the last assault at Cold Harbor was ever made. ... No advantage whatsoever was gained to compensate for the heavy loss we sustained.*

On June 12th, after losing many men, Grant finally disengaged and marched on his right flank, leaving the battlefield. Cold Harbor was a decisive Confederate victory - albeit the last one of the war. Overall, some 18,000 casualties (and more by some estimates) were suffered in this battle, with roughly 13,000 on the Union side and 5,000 on the Confederate side. Following this defeat, Grant marched his army towards the city of Petersburg, an important rail junction south of Richmond, Virginia. Lee - depending on the city for supplies of the Confederate army - raced to defend it.

At Petersburg, the Union troops were dangerously close to Richmond. The city lay just 40 kilometers south of the capital, and Grant managed to reach it before Lee and intended to occupy it. However, the Confederate forces defending the city managed to hold out just long enough until reinforcements arrived. What ensued was a grueling nine-month siege of Petersburg, the culmination of Grant's 1864 campaigning. Throughout this siege there were numerous smaller and larger skirmishes, clashes on both sides and entrenched warfare that was almost a prototype example of the later trench warfare of the Great War. But both sides dug in and widened their trenches, prolonging this attrition warfare until April of 1865. Many historians agree that this was actually a key part of Grant's overall strategy, as he wanted to gain time in order that the other Union campaigns could run smoothly and ultimately force Lee to surrender. One of the iconic moments of the Siege of Petersburg was the so-called *"Battle of the Crater"*, one of the last successes of the Confederate army in the field of battle. The crater in question was created after the Union engineers placed an immense tonnage of gunpowder into secret tunnels that ran below Confederate trenches. When the charges were exploded, they left an incredible crater that was 170 feet (52 m) long, 60 to 80 feet (24 m) wide, and 30 feet (9.1 m) deep. Thinking that the Confederate troops were dazed and devastated, the Union soldiers charged head on - but made one big mistake. Instead of flanking around the crater as they were supposed to, they ran directly into it - and were unable to exit again. What ensued was popularly called at the time a "turkey shoot" - the poor Union soldiers ran into a dead end and could not flee: they were shot down en-masse by the recuperating Confederate troops. Casualties were immense.

Still, after nine long months, Robert E. Lee was finally pressured into abandoning both Richmond and Petersburg, and retreating further to the southwest, unable to withstand the siege any longer.

Meanwhile, Ulysses Grant conducted his Valley Campaigns from May to October 1864. These campaigns were conducted in the Shenandoah Valley, and their goal was to cut off the Confederate supply lines and destroy the overall Southern economy. One of the main ways to do this was the "scorched earth" tactic.

However, not everything went according to Grant's plans for the Shenandoah campaign. General Franz Sigel - Grant's first choice for the task - led 10,000 troops south down the valley, and was soon defeated by the numerically inferior Confederate army. This happened on May 15th, 1864 during the Battle of New Market, where Confederate General John C. Breckinridge soundly defeated his troops. Sigel was soon replaced by David Hunter, a General that attracted attention with his actions, so Lee decided to send troops to restrain him. Under the leadership of Jubal Early, the Southerners had no major problems when dealing with Hunter, and shortly afterwards they moved north toward Washington. Lincoln became concerned and called Grant to come in person to defend himself - Grant sent a pair of divisions to respond. The Southerners then marched back into the Shenandoah valley, inflicting heavy damage on their opponents during the retreat. After the initial failures under Sigel and Hunter, Grant finally managed to find an adequate commander for his Shenandoah campaign. And this commander was Phillip Sheridan, with whom the North finally had a general capable of carrying out the plans outlined. After several conflicts between August and November 1864, he managed to defeat Jubal Early and began destroying the valley systematically, by burning houses, stables, mills, crops, and killing cattle. Sheridan won a string of smaller battles against the highly competent Jubal Early, and finally defeated him in a surprising Battle of Cedar Creek.

In the East, General William Tecumseh Sherman, in sync with Grant, launched his campaign which lasted from May until September 1864. As we already mentioned, the ultimate goal of the campaign was to conquer Atlanta. Sherman therefore set out from Chattanooga to invade Georgia, following in the footsteps of Joseph Johnston with his troops. There were a number of minor clashes as they made their way to Atlanta, where Sherman tried to attack Johnston's flank, sometimes resulting in heavy casualties. Johnston was eventually forced to camp in Atlanta. Jefferson Davis was concerned about the whole situation and could not allow such an important city to fall into the Union's hands. After receiving a report that Johnston was incapable of defending the city, he decided to replace him with John Bell Hood. The latter proved to be a very aggressive commander and started a direct fight with Sherman. What ensued was the Battle of Atlanta (July 22nd, 1864) - a decisive Union victory. By attacking Tecumseh Sherman, John Bell Hood suffered huge losses and was in an even worse position to defend the city. Finally, Sherman realized that Hood would have to leave the city if he destroyed the railroad, which he managed to do. Hood withdrew with his troops from the city and in retreat destroyed numerous warehouses and set fire to wagons of ammunition. Sherman refused to hunt him down - a move which many criticized as it was the main Confederate army in the west. However, he saw the importance in conquering strategic points and weakening supply opportunities rather than defeating the army itself, like Grant thought. Finally, Atlanta was conquered on September 2, 1864.

After 100 days of campaigning, Grant decided that the soldiers should at last rest, partly because he felt that the Confederacy did not have a strong enough force to defeat him. Meanwhile, John Bell Hood and the defeated Southerners were visited by Jefferson Davis.

Together, they decided that it was necessary to aggressively attack the Union's supply lines. Tecumseh Sherman tried to catch them for a while, but ultimately failed. Still, not dissuaded, he devised a different plan for the future of the campaign. This time, his goal was the city of Savannah, a coastal city in Georgia, some 400 km from Atlanta. On the way there, his army would destroy Southern infrastructure, free slaves, usurp Southern citizens, and supply themselves with whatever they could get their hands on. Lincoln and Grant did not respond best to the news of this new campaign, but Sherman persevered and was eventually approved to implement it. This military campaign was known as "Sherman's March to the Sea", and began on November 15th, 1864 with 65,000 troops involved. In general, this campaign was a clearly outlined attempt by Sherman to follow a total war "scorched earth" policy and cause a major disruption of the already frail Southern economy. In his "Special Field Orders, No. 120", Tecumseh Sherman clearly outlined the conduct for the campaign and his goals:

"... IV. The army will forage liberally on the country during the march. To this end, each brigade commander will organize a good and sufficient foraging party, under the command of one or more discreet officers, who will gather, near the route traveled, corn or forage of any kind, meat of any kind, vegetables, corn-meal, or whatever is needed by the command, aiming at all times to keep in the wagons at least ten day's provisions for the command and three days' forage. Soldiers must not enter the dwellings of the inhabitants, or commit any trespass, but during a halt or a camp they may be permitted to gather turnips, apples, and other vegetables, and to drive in stock of their camp. To regular foraging parties must be instructed the gathering of provisions and forage at any distance from the road traveled.

V. To army corps commanders alone is entrusted the power to destroy mills, houses, cotton-gins, &c., and for them this general principle is laid down: In districts and neighborhoods where the army is unmolested no destruction of such property should be permitted; but should guerrillas or bushwhackers molest our march, or should the inhabitants burn bridges, obstruct roads, or otherwise manifest local hostility, then army commanders should order and enforce a devastation more or less relentless according to the measure of such hostility.

VI. As for horses, mules, wagons, &c., belonging to the inhabitants, the cavalry and artillery may appropriate freely and without limit, discriminating, however, between the rich, who are usually hostile, and the poor or industrious, usually neutral or friendly. Foraging parties may also take mules or horses to replace the jaded animals of their trains, or to serve as pack-mules for the regiments or brigades. In all foraging, of whatever kind, the parties engaged will refrain from abusive or threatening language, and may, where the officer in command thinks proper, give written certificates of the facts, but no receipts, and they will endeavor to leave with each family a reasonable portion for their maintenance.

VII. Negroes who are able-bodied and can be of service to the several columns may be taken along, but each army commander will bear in mind that the question of supplies is a very important one and that his first duty is to see to them who bear arms...."

The Confederates noticed the movement of the Northern Army, but J. B. Hood thought it would now be easier to attack Tennessee or Kentucky, for example. Sherman divided the army into two parts so as to hide his true target, and also for the reason that Southerners would have to separate their troops as well, in order to stop them. A number of smaller battles occurred during Sherman's March to the Sea, chiefly the Battle of Griswoldville, Battle for the Doctortown Railroad Trestle, Battle of Buck Head Creek, Battle of Tulifinny, and others. Sherman eventually arrived in Savannah in early December and conquered the city without major obstacles, which brought an end to his March to Sea campaign.

The warring parties - both North and South - knew very well what their situation was in 1864. Presidential elections were held in

November, and Lincoln's success was linked to Grant's campaigns. The Confederacy, on the other hand, had to win over some of the anti-war political forces, and this was also linked to the success or failure of these campaigns. However, in the first weeks and months of these operations, Grant suffered enormous casualties, Lee successfully repulsed him, and they were eventually stuck in the siege of Petersburg. Sherman, however, did not have as many casualties, but Johnston managed to stall him, and the conquest of Atlanta dragged on. Lincoln, on the other hand, had opposition in the political ranks both outside and within his party. As already mentioned, Jubal Early managed to get close to Washington and almost won it. All this led Lincoln to believe that he would lose the election, so he wrote a letter saying that it was his duty to try to save the Union until the inauguration of the future president, because otherwise he would not be able to save it. But the scenario would soon change entirely. Democrats advocated anti-war policies and then nominated George McClellan as their candidate who in turn supported the continuation of the war. Furthermore, William Tecumseh Sherman conquered Atlanta, while Sheridan defeated Jubal Early. A huge number of Union soldiers, some of whom were not even of voting age, voted for Lincoln. The Confederacy thus lost its last chance for a possible victory.

"I Have Done My Best..."
The War's Finale and the Surrender of the Confederacy

The war was slowly coming to an end, but the Confederate leadership refused to admit it. In early 1865, only Robert E. Lee commanded significant forces, and North and South Carolina were the only states capable of supplying troops. It was these two states that were Sherman's next target, especially South Carolina, which he blamed for the outbreak of the war. Ulysses Grant planned to transport Sherman and his troops by ship, but the latter persuaded him to take an overland route. Unlike the previous campaign, this one was much more difficult because it was carried out in the winter months through swampy terrain, with unstable weather and a much poorer food supply. William Tecumseh Sherman entered South Carolina earlier that year and set fire to several cities on his way, destroying private property and railroad infrastructure - again following a scorched earth policy. North Carolina did not suffer destruction to such an extent, but the Southerners under General Johnston began to offer resistance. They clashed several times, and the struggle culminated in Sherman's victory at the Battle of Bentonville, fought from March 19th to 21st, 1865. Johnston could no longer even make a significant move, and Sherman decided to stop, rest, and resupply his troops. He wanted to avoid further casualties and end this war by maneuvering and strategy, not by battles. After a grueling nine-month siege of Richmond and Petersburg, Robert E. Lee rapidly lost manpower and supplies, so in early April of 1865 he began to retreat west in hopes of being able to resupply his forces. His once-glorious Confederate Army was now terribly thinned and desertion was rampant. It was clear that the Union armies had the clear advantage, and that the war was drawing to an end. The Confederacy made one last, desperate attempt at breaking the lasting siege of Petersburg, in a battle that was later called the "Waterloo of the Confederacy".

This battle was known as the Battle of Five Forks, and was fought on April 1st, 1865. Here, south of Petersburg, Major General Phillip Sheridan of the Union Army clashed with the numerically inferior Confederate Army commanded by Major General George Pickett. Five Forks was a key junction, and was considered "the key to control the South Side Railroad", which itself was a vital supply line and route of evacuation. Robert E. Lee understood the strategic importance of Five Forks, and thus instructed his Major General, Pickett, to defend the location at all costs. However, the battle was marked by a number of obstructions on the Confederate side, mainly an acoustic shadow that prevented Pickett from hearing the opening stages of the battle. Soon after, Union forces of Sheridan succeeded in pinning down the front and right flanks of the Confederate lines, and the left flank was also attacked soon after. The battle ended as a decisive Union victory, with high casualties on the Confederate side. On the following day Ulysses Grant ordered a full scale assault on the westward-fleeing Confederates, and Robert E. Lee had no other choice than to abandon Petersburg and the capital, Richmond. With the Confederate capital now lost, the defeat of the Confederacy was imminent, with Lee fleeing to the west. On April 3rd, Abraham Lincoln visited Richmond, Virginia, where he entered as a victor and was greeted by masses of freed African slaves that greeted him as their saviour and messiah.

The last major conflict between Grant and Lee took place on April 6th, 1854, at the Sayler's Creek battle and lasted a very short time, with the Union army capturing about 8,000 Southerners. Lee fled westwards, hoping to reconnect with Johnston's forces. Instead, he soon found himself surrounded by the Union troops. This resulted in Lee's final fight at Sayler's Creek. The battle was one of desperation, and achieved literally nothing, except the loss of 8,000 Confederate soldiers. Seeing the chaos around him, Robert E. Lee famously asked:

"My God, has the army dissolved?" His General, Mahone, answered dutifully: *"No, General, here are troops ready to do their duty."*

Lee's tattered and defeated army continued its retreat. It was now clear that the Confederacy was defeated. Lee remarked, facing the facts, that *"here is nothing left for me to do but to go and see General Grant, and I would rather die a thousand deaths."*

Soon after Sayler's Creek, Union forces completely surrounded Lee near the village of Appomattox Court House. After just a brief engagement, Lee at last realized that all hope was lost: the war was over. Finally, on April 9th, 1865, Lee and Grant met at the home of the salesman Wilmer McLean and discussed the terms of the Confederate surrender. Ulysses Grant was magnanimous in his victory. He allowed Confederate troops to keep their sidearms and horses, and he also gave the starved Confederate troops Union army rations. Robert E. Lee, addressing his faithful troops for the very last time, said:

"After four years' arduous service, marked by unsurpassed courage and fortitude, the Army of Northern Virginia has been compelled to yield to overwhelming numbers and resources. Boys, I have done the best I could for you. Go home now, and if you make as good citizens as you have soldiers, you will do well, and I shall always be proud of you."

He advised his troops and all Southern citizens to avoid the continuation of the conflicts. Lee's surrender was the effective end of the American Civil War - the loss of an army gave zero chances to the South for their cause. Jefferson Davis, fleeing southwards, pressured the Confederacy to fight on and spoke of a new phase of the struggle - even though he had no viable means to do so. Luckily, most Southerners heeded Robert E. Lee's advice and showed no interest in a guerrilla war. Most realized that continuing to fight would be futile and largely suicidal. Davis was captured on May 10th, 1865. General Johnston surrendered on April 18th, and by May 26th all other Confederate forces followed suit. The very last skirmish of the war was fought in

Texas on May 13th, in the Battle of Palmito Hill, which was - *ironically* - a Confederate victory.

Just days after the war ended, a shocking event thundered out throughout the country. Exactly four years after the lowering of the Union flag in Fort Sumter, United States - but also the rest of the world - were shaken by the news of a vicious murder. Abraham Lincoln, the President of the United States, was assasinated. John Wilkes Booth, a well-known theater actor and an ardent supporter of the Confederacy was the perpetrator. He hated Lincoln with a passion as well as his policies, and regretted the abolition of slavery which had become officially the Thirteenth Amendment. He felt like a "slave" in the North and began to hate himself for not participating in the war on the Confederate side. He learned that Lincoln would be present at a play at the Ford Theater in Washington on April 14th, 1865. With two other men, he planned to assassinate Lincoln, Vice President Andrew Johnson and Secretary of State William Seward at the same time. Booth sneaked into the theater box and shot Lincoln in the back of the head, while the other two failed to kill their targets. He jumped out of the box, shouted "*Sic Semper Tyrannis*" ("thus always to tyrants" or "so tyrants end") and fled the theater. Lincoln passed away the next morning, and Booth was found and killed on April 26th while hiding in a barn in Virginia.

A Summary of the Key Battles of the American Civil War

As we already mentioned, the American Civil War is a war of great historic significance. But one of its most challenging aspects is the sheer number of battles that were fought during those critical four years. Modern estimates agree that there were roughly 10,500 military engagements during the war in total, with 50 of these being major, turning-point battles, and over 100 being considered as significant battles. Needless to say, it would be a near-impossible task to mention even a part of these major battles in a single book. During the course of our Civil War summarization, we touched upon only the most critical and famous of battles: Gettysburg, Antietam, Chancelorssville, and such. However, it would be an injustice to the significance of this war and the number of troops lost, if we'd completely fail to mention some of the other major battles. In the following part of the book, we will offer a critical summary of some of these battles, as they can be vital for the understanding of the overall progress of the American Civil War.

- ***Battle of Wilson's Creek, August 10, 1861***

One of the early major battles of the Civil War, the Battle of Wilson's Creek (known also as the Battle of Oak Hills), was the first battle to be fought in the so-called "Trans-Mississippi Theater". It occurred on August 10th, 1861, close to Springfield, Missouri. At the time, Missouri was officially a neutral state. However, its governor, Claiborne Fox Jackson, secretly supported the Southern cause and worked with the Confederate troops. The battle was opened by the Confederate army, marching from Arkansas under the command of Brigadier General Ben McCulloch and Major General Sterling Price of the Missouri forces. They faced the troops of Brigadier General

Nathaniel Lyon and Colonel Franz Sigel, which were camped near Springfield.

On August 10th, at dawn, Nathaniel Lyon split his Union troops in two columns, him leading one and Sigel the other. They jointly attacked the Confederate troops at the position of Wilson's Creek, located some 12 miles southwest of Springfield. It was a very close battle, with neither side having a clear upper hand, even though the Confederates were numerically superior, fielding some 12, 000 men to the Union's 5,500.

As the battle unfolded, the Confederates counterattacked three times but failed to penetrate Union lines. The decisive change came about with the heroic death of the Union commander, Nathaniel Lyon. Surrounded by Confederate troops on his own, wounded in the leg and head, it is said that Lyon fought on even without weapons, throwing rocks at Confederate troops before being shot dead. He was replaced by Major Samuel Sturgis. In the meantime, Franz Sigel's column collapsed under Confederate advances. The Southerners were now able to consolidate their forces and face the remaining Union troops. Replacing Lyon, Major Sturgis now realized that his troops were exhausted and low on ammunition. He promptly ordered a full retreat to Springfield. Even though they were victorious, the Confederate forces had no means to pursue the enemy. The victory was significant in many ways. Most notably, it gave the Confederates control of the southwestern Missouri, and strengthened Confederate sympathies in this state. The Battle of Wilson's Creek was the most important event in 1861, west of the Mississippi River.

• *Battle of Pea Ridge (Battle of Elkhorn Tavern), March 7–8, 1862*

The Battle of Pea Ridge took place between March 6 and 8 in Benton Country, Arkansas. The Union forces, under the command of Brigadier General Samuel R. Curtis, faced off against the Confederates commanded by General Earl Van Dorn. The Union forces numbered some 10,400 men, while the Confederate forces had some 16,400. The battle ensued from the attempt by General Van Dorn to launch a determined Confederate counter-offensive, which would help him to recapture parts of Northern Arkansas and Missouri. The Confederate strategy for this battle as part of the Missouri winter campaign was to advance north through Missouri to try to capture St. Louis, which would help them to control the state and the Mississippi River - a key strategic asset. Van Dorn had high hopes for his counterattack. He needed to move swiftly in order to succeed and surprise the Northerners, and for that he decided on a risky move: to place his supply trains far to the rear. However, the Union leader, Samuel R. Curtis, leading his Army of the Southwest, learned of this risky approach and at once marched his troops to meet the Confederates in battle. The two parties clashed at the site called Elkhorn Tavern, not more than three miles south of the Missouri border. A vicious clash ensued. On the first day of the battle, the Confederates made some moderate success, gaining control of two key positions: the Telegraph Road and Elkhorn Tavern. However, during the night lull, Brigadier General Curtis consolidated his troops and counterattacked. With cunning use of artillery, Curtis managed to push the Confederates back. Eventually, Van Dorn disengaged, and the Battle of Pea Ridge ended as a decisive Union victory. One of the key aspects of the Confederate defeat was their lack of supplies, since Van Dorn decided to leave his supply train too far back. Also critical was a major loss of morale and momentum amongst the Confederates, since two renowned Brigadier Generals were killed during the battle - Ben McCulloch and James McQueen. Van Dorn's defeat left the territory of Arkansas practically defenseless. Pea Ridge was important in many ways, since with this victory, the Union gained control of the Missouri border for the next two years of the war. The casualties in this clash were moderately high, with the Confederates suffering some 2,000 dead, wounded, and missing, and the Union troops suffering roughly 203 killed, 1000 wounded, and 200 missing.

Another interesting fact related to this battle is the use of some 2,000 Native American troops, predominantly Cherokee, on the Confederate side. They fought in their traditional manner and in the native way. This was the first sizable Civil War battle, where Native Americans fought. Did you know that the last Confederate General to surrender in the American Civil War was a Native American? His name was Brigadier-General Stand Watie, also known as Tawkertawker, a Cherokee leader that commanded the Native American troops composed of Cherokee, Seminole, and Muskogee Indians.

• *Battle of Shiloh, April 6–7, 1862*

One of the foremost engagements of the early Civil War, the Battle of Shiloh (also known as the Battle of Pittsburg Landing) was the one clash that left the United States stunned, and offered a view into the future of the war. The battle was fought between 6th and 7th April, 1862, in Hardin County, Tennessee. On the Union side, the commanders were Major General Ulysses S. Grant and General Major Don Carlos Buell, and they commanded a major force of some 63,000 men. Opposing them were the Confederates, led by Generals Albert Sydney Johnston and P. G. T. Beauregard, who commanded the Army of Mississippi that was roughly 40,500 strong.

Grant decided to move deeper into Tennessee, following the flow of the Tennessee River. Grant encamped near Pittsburg Landing on the river's west bank. Albery Sydney Johnston started the Battle of Shiloh with a surprise attack on the Union army, greatly shocking Grant. What ensued was a brutal fight that claimed many lives. Johnston hoped to swiftly defeat Grant, knowing that additional Union troops were arriving to reinforce him. However, the skilled Confederate leader, Albert S. Johnston was killed during the early fighting, and had to be replaced by Beauregard, who took command of the troops.

Beauregard was well known (especially in the later stages of the Civil War) as an indecisive and overly cautious commander. Upon taking control of the troops, he at once decided *against* pressing an attack in the late evening. This allowed Ulysses Grant to recuperate overnight and to receive reinforcements in the form of four additional divisions. With this, the Union army launched a surprising and decisive counterattack in the early morning, completely turning the tide of the battle. One of the main Union positions in the battle, nicknamed the "Hornet's Nest", offered such fierce resistance against the enemy, and it allowed the rest of the Union troops to stabilize and reassemble. When Grant received his reinforcements, he quickly launched a full-on counterattack along the *entire line*. The Confederates stood no chance, and Beauregard was forced to retreat. Their defeat meant that the Union advance into Northern Mississippi could no longer be staved off.

The Battle of Shiloh was the most destructive and bloodiest battle in the Civil War up to that point. It took the general public by storm, and many were shocked that the war opened with such brutality. The Union army - even though they won - suffered higher casualties than the Confederates. Furthermore, Ulysses S. Grant - who would go on to have a stellar Civil War record - was highly criticized in Washington for being surprised by Albert Sydney Johnston.

Overall, the Union side suffered some 13,047 casualties, of which some 1,754 were killed, 8,408 wounded, and roughly 3,000 captured and missing. In comparison, the Confederates had 10,699 casualties, of which 1,728 died, 8,000 were wounded, and some 1,000 were captured or missing. Shiloh is important for the fact that it had nearly twice as many casualties as the previous major battles of the war combined.

- ***Battle of Stones River (Second Battle of Murfreesboro), December 31, 1862 – January 2, 1863***

The Second Battle of Murfreesboro was one of the most important Civil War engagements, especially for the Union side. It saw the Union Major General William Rosecrans - who was eager to prove himself - pitting his 43,400-strong army against the Confederate troops under Braxton Bragg, numbering some 35,000 men.

Following the Battle of Perryville on October 8th, 1862, which was a slim Union victory, the Union Major General Don Carlos Buell could not effectively follow up and exploit this win. Abraham Lincoln, displeased by his lack of results, soon replaced him with Major General William S. Rosecrans, giving him command of the Army of Ohio, soon to be renamed Army of the Cumberland. William Rosecrans had a lot to prove to Lincoln. This was all the more apparent with the preliminary Emancipation Proclamation, which Lincoln issued on September 22nd, 1862. Because of this, Lincoln *needed* and expected his troops to achieve as many victories against the Confederates as possible, in order to give the Emancipation Proclamation the much needed "backbone" and approval.

In late 1862, the newly formed Army of the Cumberland under Rosecrans marched south from Nashville, Tennessee, towards Murfreesboro, where they were to clash with the Confederates under Braxton Bragg. Rosecrans entered into the fray overly cautious: he left some 40,000 men around Nashville in order to protect his supply and communication lines. Braxton Bragg saw this as a clear advantage. Thus, he was the first to attack - launching a massive assault against the Union right flank at Stones River. Initially repulsed and broken, the Union troops managed to assemble a defensive line and repulse repeated piecemeal Confederate attacks. This, and numerous other mistakes on the Confederate side, led to the battle ending as a Union victory. Braxton Bragg, falsely believing that William Rosecrans was about to receive additional reinforcements, ordered a full retreat on January 3rd.

This was the victory that Lincoln wanted, and it gave the Union control of Central Tennessee, as well as an important morale boost, especially after the disaster at Fredericksburg in late 1862. Lincoln knew well enough that this victory was barely achieved, and wrote to William Rosecrans: *"...you gave us a hard victory which, had there been a defeat instead, the nation could scarcely have lived over."*

The Second Battle of Murfreesboro was another slaughterhouse of the Civil War, with casualties being some of the highest in the war. The percentage of casualties was in fact higher than the Battles of Shiloh and Antietam. The Union troops had some 13,000 casualties, including roughly 1,700 killed, 7,500 wounded, and around 3,500 captured and missing. For the Confederates, these numbers were only marginally lower, with 11,700 casualties in total, of which 1,300 were killed, up to 8,000 wounded, and some 2,500 captured and missing. Also, four brigadier generals lost their lives in this battle. One interesting fact related to the Second Battle of Murfreesboro is related to Frances Elizabeth Quinn, a female Union soldier that disguised herself as a man in order to fight. She was wounded in this battle, but lived.

• *Battle of Chickamauga, September 18–20, 1863*

Arguably one of the most famous battles of the American Civil War, the Battle of Chickamauga once again pitted William Rosecrans and Braxton Bragg against one another. Fought from September 18th to 20th, 1863, this clash was centered on the small town of Chattanooga on the banks of the Tennessee River. However, Chattanooga was no ordinary town: it was at the crossroads of four major railroads. Lincoln quickly realized that if his troops were to capture Chattanooga, they would deal a hard blow on the Confederates, cutting off their vital supply routes. Rosecrans, who once already dealt a blow on Braxton Bragg at the Second Battle of Murfreesboro, was now feeling confident and ambitious. He led an offensive and quickly forced Bragg out of Chattanooga, pursuing him south. Commanding his Confederate Army of Tennessee, Braxton Bragg was determined to clash with Rosecrans, defeat him, and recapture Chattanooga. But what Rosecrans assumed was that the Southerners were to continue fleeing all the way to Rome in Georgia. To that end, he split his army into three parts, making a critical mistake. Braxton Bragg concentrated all his men nearer to LaFayette in Georgia, and was quite close to one of Rosecrans' weaker corps. Furthermore, he awaited reinforcements as well. And once Braxton Bragg crossed the river known as Chickamauga Creek, he opened the decisive Battle of Chickamauga. What ensued was a vicious two-day battle that had some of the highest casualty rates in the entire war. With the fight drawing on, Bragg realized that his initial plan of swiftly retaking Chattanooga would not come to pass. Instead, he decided to besiege the city from nearby heights. During the critical stages of this battle, William Rosecrans - whose military record was commendable up to that point - made a crucial error. Hoping to bridge a supposed gap in his ranks, he maneuvered a part of his troops in such a way as to create an actual wide gap in his lines. This gap was directly in the path of a Confederate assault led by Lieutenant General James Longstreet, whose attack decisively drove one third of the Union army - as well as Rosecrans - from the battlefield.

The remnants of the Union army managed to hold on until twilight, when they at last retreated to the city of Chattanooga. The Confederates were victorious, and continued their siege of the town. However, just two months later, a series of clashes began, known as the Battles for Chattanooga. Union leader Ulysses Grant sent reinforcements and ultimately drove the Confederate Army of Tennessee into a retreat, permanently securing Chattanooga for the North. In the end, it made the southern victory at Chickamauga redundant, and a strategic defeat on a larger scale.

As far as casualties are concerned, the Battle of Chickamauga reached the highest number of losses of any battle in the Western

Theater of the American Civil War. The battle saw roughly 125,000 men deployed on both sides. Of these, the Union troops suffered some 16,000 casualties (1,700 killed, around 10,000 wounded, and nearly 5,000 missing and captured). The Confederates suffered almost 19,000 casualties, with 2,100 killed, almost 15,000 wounded, and roughly 1,500 captured or missing. It was a vicious bloodshed, from which both sides would take a long time to recuperate. Furthermore, some 10 Confederate Generals were killed and wounded in this battle.

The Union defeat at Chickamauga effectively ended the military career of William S. Rosecrans.

• *Battle of Chancellorsville, April 30–May 6, 1863*

Arguably the most famous and important battle of the American Civil War - at least for the Confederate side - the Battle of Chancellorsville took America by surprise. A culminating point of the Chancellorsville Campaign, the battle was fought from April 30th to May 6th, 1863, in Spotsylvania County in Virginia. It was the true "duel of the fates", and saw a vastly numerically superior Union army under the command of Major General Joseph Hooker, facing off against Robert E. Lee's outnumbered Army of Northern Virginia. What ensued was a devastating battle that displayed the true marvel and ability of Robert E. Lee, as he won a decisive victory in what was called his "perfect battle".

Preceding this battle was a heavy clash at Fredericksburg in the winter of 1862-1863, one of the war's major turning points. However, when the Union commander, Hooker, decided to secretly transfer the greater part of his army up the banks of the Rappahannock River and then cross it in late April 1863, he set the stage for a major confrontation - one that has been criticized by many. Simultaneously with Hooker's crossing of the Rappahannock, the Union cavalry under Major General George Stoneman, began raiding Robert E. Lee's supply lines - to practically no effect. By April 30th, the Union infantry was concentrated near the city of Chancellorsville, after crossing the Rapidan River. Hooker commanded a vast army numbering close to 134,000. Together with his troops at Fredericksburg, he planned to do a "double envelopment" and defeat Lee by attacking him from both front and rear. However, Robert E. Lee made a risk of a lifetime, a gambit that took everyone by surprise. On May 1st, as Hooker moved in from Chancellorsville to attack Lee, the latter split his army into two forces in the face of superior numbers. He left one-fifth of the Confederate army at Fredericksburg to halt the Union advance there, and took the remaining four-fifths to attack the advance troops of Joseph Hooker. The first of Hooker's many mistakes occurred at this point: he ordered his troops to retreat to the defensive lines closer to Chancellorsville, ignoring the objections by his subordinate officers. By doing this, Hooker lost the initiative and instead gave it over to Robert E. Lee. Robert K. Krick, in his famed work "Lee's Greatest Victory", writes:

> *"Lee's Chancellorsville consisted of a pastiche of unbelievably risky gambits that led to a great triumph. Hooker's campaign, after the brilliant opening movements, degenerated into a tale of opportunities missed and troops underutilized."*

Another one of these gambits by Lee happened on May 2nd, when he once more split his troops into two. He sent an entire corps commanded by Stonewall Jackson - his most trusted General - to conduct a flanking attack that succeeded in routing the entire XI Corps of the Union forces. By the next day, the battle erupted in earnest, with some of the fiercest fighting occurring. May 3rd has been called the second bloodiest day of the entire American Civil War - and that it was. Robert E. Lee launched several successive assaults on the Union troops at Chancellorsville. BOth sides suffered immense losses, while the main bulk of Joseph Hooker's army pulled back. At the same time, the remaining Union troops under Major General John Sedgwick advanced across the Rappahannock River and defeated the

Confederates at the Second Battle of Fredericksburg (Marye's Heights). Due to this, Robert E. Lee continued his gambits and gambles: he turned his back to Hooker, attacked John Sedgwick, defeated him, and surrounded the Union troops on three sides. With Sedgwick retreating across the river on May 5th, Lee could once again turn back to confront Hooker. The latter retreated across the river by May 6th. With the campaign concluded, Lee quickly reorganized his army and just one month later began his Gettysburg Campaign. Chancellorsville was a decisive and important Confederate Victory. It was marked with Lee's brilliance, audacity, and his many successful risks, as well as with Joseph Hooker's slowed decision-making and too much caution. The battle ended with heavy casualties on both sides, and also with the loss of one of the finest Confederate Generals: Thomas "Stonewall" Jackson. While conducting reconnaissance in advance of his own lines, after dark, Stonewall Jackson was hit by friendly fire. He was wounded in his left arm, which had to be quickly amputated. Just eight days later, the legend that was Stonewall Jackson died of pneumonia and the resulting complications. Robert E. Lee was devastated by this loss, as Stonewall was one of his most competent subordinates. Upon hearing the news, a crushed Lee said to his personal cook: *"William, I have lost my right arm. I'm bleeding at the heart."* Stonewall Jackson is widely hailed as one of the best Confederate commanders.

● *Siege of Vicksburg, May 18 – July 4, 1863*

The Siege of Vicksburg undoubtedly marked the year of 1863. It was the final engagement and the culmination of the Vicksburg Campaign, and one of the important victories of the Union Major General Ulysses S. Grant. The Siege of Vicksburg took place in Warren County, Mississippi, close to the city of Vicksburg. It was fought between May 18th and July 4th, 1863. Ulysses Grant commanded his Union Army of Tennessee that numbered roughly 77,000 men, and faced the Confederates under Lieutenant General John C. Pemberton, who commanded just 33,000 men. In a series of skilled military maneuvers, Ulysses Grant proved his competence when he crossed the Mississippi River and drove the Confederates under Pemberton to retreat into defensive positions around the fortress city of Vicksburg. This city was a vital point for the Confederates - being their last stronghold on the Mississippi. Both Lincoln and Grant understood how important its capture was. But taking it would be no easy task. The Confederates were well defended, and two major assaults by Grant's troops ended in failure and with incredibly high casualties. Due to this, Grant decided on a different strategy. He would besiege the city, cutting off their supplies and starving the garrison. What ensued was nearly two months of grueling siege and mutual artillery shelling that left many dead on both sides. The Confederates bravely held out for more than 40 days, but their supplies were running critically low in the end. With no food for either the troops or the civilians living in Vicksburg, the Confederate commander Pemberton was forced to surrender the city on July 4th, 1863. His only condition for surrender was that his men were to be released.

Grant's victory at Vicksburg successfully completed the Vicksburg Campaign and dealt a major blow to the Confederates and their war effort. It gave the Northerners the command of the Mississippi River, a major strategic asset. Vicksburg greatly hampered the Confederate ability to maintain their war. Because of this, as well as the Confederate defeat at Gettysburg (which happened a day before the surrender at Vicksburg), Vicksburg is considered a turning point of the American Civil War. Abraham Lincoln famously called this victory "the key to the war". Furthermore, it was Vicksburg that greatly strengthened Grant's growing reputation.

Casualties in this siege were notoriously one-sided. The Union forces suffered "only" around 766 killed, and around 4,000 wounded. In comparison, the besieged Confederates suffered around 3,200 wounded, killed, and missing in total, with some 29,500 troops surrendering in the aftermath. Did you know that one of the Confederate casualties in the Siege of Vicksburg was a *camel*? Douglas the Camel, known as "Old Douglas", was a Dromedary Camel in service with the 43rd Mississippi Infantry. An important mascot for the regiment, the camel also was a part of the regimental band, carrying instruments and supplies. Old Douglas was greatly loved by the troops, and was known as a "faithful and patient" camel that never wandered far from the soldiers. Interestingly, the camel was in active service during the 1862 Battles of Iuka, and the Battle of Corinth. During the Siege of Vicksburg, however, Old Douglas was killed by a Union sharpshooter. This greatly enraged the Confederate troops and battered their morale, and they swore to avenge him. A special grave marker dedicated to Old Douglas the Camel exists at the Cedar Hill Cemetery, in Vicksburg, Mississippi.

"Mending a Torn-Apart Nation"
The Reconstruction Period: 1865-1877

After four years of vicious, brother-on-brother warfare, the long sought-after peace finally settled upon the United States. It took a lot of bloodshed and a lot of innocent lives lost to finally see whose ideology was to prevail in the American Civil War. Alas, these four years of conflict did not fail to leave a mark upon America. The civilian population of the war torn areas - especially in the South - was exhausted, displaced, and devastated. Entire cities were damaged and burned, the crops plundered, villages razed and raided. These effects were particularly strong during the Union invasion of the South under William Tecumseh Sherman, whose "scorched earth" policies terribly destroyed the Southern economy and morale. And now, after the war ended, it was time to rebuild America anew, to heal wounds and mend differences, beginning a fresh new journey of a war-torn nation. It was now time to ask the burning question: how, and under which conditions, will the Southern states be incorporated into the Union again. This question - and many - others, were answered and realized in the decade that followed the war, in the so-called "Reconstruction period". In fact, the reconstruction period began even as the war raged on, but intensified after 1865. It was the idea of Abraham Lincoln, who envisioned the reconstruction as early as 1863. Alas, the assassination that deprived him of life also deprived him of the chance to fulfill his visions of a different America. The first step of the reconstruction was the Emancipation Proclamation, which Lincoln delivered early in the war. This was followed by the Proclamation of Amnesty and Reconstruction - better known as the Ten Percent Plan - which Lincoln introduced in December of 1863. Lincoln wanted to mend the Union as quickly as possible, and to strengthen the Republicans in the South - if possible. His plan saw the amnesty and the return of private property to everyone in the South, except the highest officials of the Confederation. Also planned was to allow the establishment of a new government when 10% of the voters would announce loyalty to the Union, and also to allow the states themselves to plan what to do with the freed slaves - as long as their freedom was not affected. Radical Republicans strongly protested these decisions, considering that Abraham Lincoln was too lenient towards the South. This is why, in the summer of 1864, the Republicans backed the Wade-Davis Bill, which demanded that 50% of the voters announce their loyalty, and the freed slaves to have protection under the law and the right to vote (a thing seen as scandalous in the South).

However, this was vetoed by Lincoln and the plans of the Republicans quickly collapsed. Still, the Congress had a say in the reconstruction plan after the death of Lincoln. The latter was afraid of the post-war scenario in which the freedom of the slaves would not last, and thus did his best to make sure that these freedoms would be guaranteed. That is exactly how the famed Thirteenth Amendment came to be, with the goal of completely forbidding slavery.

After it was voted in the Senate, ratification abruptly stopped in the House of Representatives because the Democrats voted against it. However, the Republicans were strengthened after Lincoln's victory in the 1864 elections, and even managed to win over some Democrats. The only remaining step was to send an amendment to the states and await ratification, which was not realized until December of 1865. The post-war reconstruction took place in two parts, the first part led by Lincoln's successor, Andrew Johnson, and the second part led by radical Republicans.

The late Abraham Lincoln was succeeded by Andrew Johnson, a Democrat who was of the opinion that reconstruction was his job. He appointed interim governors to some southern states, granted pardons to Confederate army officials who requested them, and provided guidance to southern leaders for elections and re-accession to the

Union. Thus, many individuals regained influential positions in, for example, politics or economics, regardless of their support for the Confederacy. They did not guarantee the civil rights of ex-slaves or allow ex-slaves to participate in political life. Furthermore, most Southern states began to establish a new socio-economic system in the form of laws called the "Black Codes", which aimed to limit the freedom and political power of former slaves and provide cheap labor. The situation began to look worryingly similar to the structure of slavery. Many Republicans initially supported Johnson's plans, except for radicals who were angry at the lenient policies and refusal to recognize the right to vote of African Americans. Southerners have managed to get several seats in Congress because now one African-American counted as one person, not as three-fifths of one person as has been the case so far. As early as March 1865, Lincoln, with the help of the Congress, established the Freedmen's Bureau (1865-1872). The agency included many associations whose goal was to provide education, accommodation, mediation in concluding employment contracts, assistance and advice on legal matters, and the provision of basic necessities such as food and medicine. Furthermore, they built hospitals, colleges and universities, and achieved less success in civil rights.

President Johnson felt that the agency's activities were too broad and that it prevented former slaves from becoming independent. Democrats were against the agency because they believed that everyone who receives help becomes lazy. There was also a wave of violence throughout the former Confederate states, creating the Ku Klux Klan in Tennessee, whose members often and brutally used violence against African Americans. They realized that it was more important for him to annex the southern states back to the Union than the rights of African Americans, so they decided to use their power to protect them. The President and the Democrats opposed the amendment, but failed to prevent the ratification that took place in July 1866.

It was quickly becoming apparent to the new President Johnson that the Congress was hastily taking the reconstruction into its own hands. In the past, he had been a prominent Unionist in the South. But soon after, he favored the ex-Confederates and became the leading opponent of freedmen and their Radical Republicans allies. To that end, he continued his policies and struggles and continually disturbed the Republicans and their intentions.

The elections of 1866 decisively changed the balance of power in America, giving the Radical Republicans two-thirds majorities in both houses of Congress, and enough votes to overcome Johnson's vetoes. Furthermore, by 1866, the Radical Republicans were convinced that Johnson's faction and his Southern appointees were disloyal to the Union and hostile to the freedmen. They thought that the reconstruction should be started anew, and to that end they began a fierce political struggle with the Democrats, creating many new laws. After Johnson protested and vetoed the proposed laws, Republicans rejected it and passed the First Reconstruction Act of 1867. This law established five military zones in the territory of the former Confederacy, and each was headed by a federal general. The new delegates were to write a new Constitution in each state and put it to the vote. All adult men, with the exception of those who actively supported the Confederacy and convicts, were given the right to vote. Any state wishing to rejoin the Union had to ratify the Fourteenth Amendment first and only then could it send representatives to Congress. Johnson did not give up in the fight against the Republicans, deliberately obstructing their every move. However, his popularity was declining, and the Republicans tried unsuccessfully to remove him.

He managed to preserve his presidential position, but he stopped interfering with Republican plans. The Reconstruction kept on rolling, and great successes were made for the Afro-Americans and their cause. With the ratification of the Fifteenth Amendment in 1870, the voting rights for American citizens were no longer dependent on skin color.

Many black Americans were now an active part of voting in new amendments in the Southern states, where just a few years before they were treated as slaves and not persons. Some African-Americans even entered into politics, such as Hiram Revels and Blanche K. Bruce in Mississippi, both of whom became senators.

In the South, reconstruction led to the influx of Northerners who saw a chance to profit in the newly created situation and circumstances. They also had an intention to actively contribute to the political future of these states. A special derogatory term for these opportunistic Northerners who had no local connections in the South emerged in the post-war years: *carpetbagger.* Another slur originated in the South at that time: *scalawag.* This was used to denote white Southerners who were supportive of the Republicans in their states and of the Reconstruction as a whole. These parties together made the foundation of Republican power in the former Confederate states.

Johnson was succeeded in 1868 by Ulysses S. Grant who joined up with the Republicans and for the next few years worked closely with them on the reconstruction process. However, during Grant's second term, the four states that rejoined the Union were controlled by white Southerners, better known as the Redeemers. Sadly, as a consequence of the influence of the Republicans, Carpetbaggers, and Scalawags, the Democratic Party was strengthened, but so was the racist Ku Klux Klan, which emerged in 1866 and operated as a paramilitary organization. The Ku Klux Klan members (or clansmen) wore white robes and hoods, and their goal was to restore the power of whites in the states of the former Confederacy. They were considered a radical and racist organization, who even killed and wounded African-Americans, lynching them and burning their houses and churches. Whites were also a target for them, especially those that voted Republican. Due to this, the Congress delivered three special acts, all with the intention to stop violence. The "First Enforcement Act" forbade the wearing of the distinct white hoods and robes of the Ku Klux Klan, while the "Second Enforcement Act" allowed state agents to observe the votings across the South. Even so, violence continued in the South. Grant reacted by creating the "Third Enforcement Act", also known as the "Ku Klux Klan Act". This new act proclaimed it a federal crime to disrupt voting, political business, and other disruptions. While all this curbed the violence, it did not stop it entirely. As conflicts mounted, the Ku Klux Klan was almost entirely destroyed, while the freed African-Americans in the South still had a largely restricted access to voting and political life. All this allowed the Southern Democrats to gradually regain the power that they have lost over the years. In 1876, new elections were held. And even though Grant wanted to continue his mandate, some of the Republicans blocked his nomination. The 1876 Elections were marked by a controversy surrounding the results, so the Congress had to declare the winner. This was the Republican candidate, Rutherford B. Hayes, who served as the 19th president of the United States, from 1877 to 1881. Still, the Democrats did not allow them to fully prevail and manipulate the political system: they were more concerned with the finalization of the Reconstruction period and the self-governing of the states. In 1877, the Congress members agreed on a compromise, known as the "Compromise of 1877". This "unwritten deal" declared the Civil War finally "put to rest". The Democrats acknowledged the decision of the Congress in relation to the Election of Rutherford B. Hayes, and the new president in response removed the Federal troops from South Carolina, Florida, and Louisiana. After the army left these states, the African-American politicians were promptly relieved of their positions, and the rights of African-Americans in general were disrupted in many ways - for example, through taxation of voting. Soon after, the so-called "Jim Crow Laws" were ushered in across the south. These laws opened a dark era of disenfranchisement and legal racial segregation. It dictated that "colored persons" (i.e. African-Americans) had to be physically separated from white people in almost all places in society, especially in public transport and schools. These controversial laws of segregation were in force until the middle of the 20th century, when a movement for human rights quickly spread throughout the United States with great success.

"The Mute Witnesses of History" Casualties of the American Civil War

Wars are unforgiving. No conflict in the history of mankind was ever lenient towards men and women, both fighting and observing. Each war, each bullet fired, has long lasting and far reaching consequences. Like a ripple through time, a single fired bullet can shake lives and change destinies. The American Civil War was no exception. It was one of the bloodiest conflicts of its time - a devastating war that filled a short span of four years with so much bloodshed and death. In a military aspect, it was a war both archaic and modern - somewhere right in the middle of the two. Archaic strategies and tactics led directly to many casualties, while the more modern war technologies contributed equally to the mass bloodshed. Due to all this, the American Civil War was one of the bloodiest conflicts of the 19th century - and one that had the world watch in mute horror as the fate of a nation was decided anew.

In this section we will take a deeper look into the casualties that his war produced. It is undoubtedly the most touching aspect of every war, but one that we still need to address in order to produce a detailed and all-encompassing portrayal of this crucial piece of American history. One of the foremost authors to deal with the casualties numbers in the postwar years was a Civil War veteran, Thomas L. Livermore (1844-1918). His most influential piece of work is without a doubt *"Numbers and Losses in the Civil War in America 1861-65"* (published in 1901), which is widely regarded as the standard reference work for statistics about Civil War unit strengths and casualties. The author conducted extensive research on this tricky subject, giving us a detailed look into the striking number of men and women that suffered in this war.

Livermore pointed out that he did not hope that his data were complete, given the possible mistakes he made and the incomplete (or destroyed) military records. Namely, the author states that the total number of Union soldiers in the war was 2,898,304, while the Confederacy deployed about 600,000 to 700,000 soldiers, believing that this number is certainly higher due to the already mentioned shortcomings in the research. Also contributing to the higher Confederate numbers could be many volunteer, guerilla, and other forces. Another vital source is the U.S. National Park Service, which tells us that there were 2,672,341 Union soldiers active in the war, of which 2,489,836 were whites, 178,975 African Americans and 3,530 North American Indians. Confederate figures are estimated at approximately 750,000 to 1,227,890.

As for the victims, the figure of about 1,030,000 casualties is usually mentioned, of which about 620,000 are dead. But in 2011, in a study by David Hacker, a historian at Binghamton University, we can find a figure of 750,000 deaths. He claims that neither the Union nor the Confederation kept standardized records of staff. James McPherson, a noted Civil War historian, agreed that the figure was certainly greater than 620,000, and that Hacker's results were the result of the unreported deaths of Confederate soldiers. The National Park Service lists the total number of casualties as follows: 642,427 Union soldiers and 483,026 Confederate soldiers, or a total of 1,125,509 casualties.

It is important to note that not all of the dead were victims of brutal combat. Many soldiers succumbed to the ravages of disease and hunger and elements, often in greater proportions than in combat. The U.S. National Park Service records tell us that on the Union side, from a total of 853,838 casualties, some 110,100 were killed in action, while roughly 224,580 were disease deaths. Also listed are 275,154 soldiers wounded in action and 211,411 captured (including 30,192 who died as prisoners of war). On the other side, the Confederate losses are listed at 914,660, of which 94,000 were killed in action and 164,000 were disease deaths. Continuing, there were some 194,026 troops wounded in action, and an immense 462,634 captured (including 31,000 who died as prisoners of war). All of this provides a critical glimpse into the ravages and brutality of this war.

Another problematic aspect of the casualties of the American Civil War is the number of former slaves that have perished. These deaths were much more difficult to estimate, especially because reliable census data was seriously lacking at the time, as well as because of racial prejudice and discrimination. During the war itself, a "no mercy policy" and massacres against former slaves and African-American Union troops were not unheard of, and this may have contributed to inconclusive estimates. Former slave deaths due to disease, malnourishment, and exposure could have been very hight at the time, especially considering the fact that many African slaves fled persecution and escaped to Union territories in great numbers. However, en route there, and once they arrived, they faced insufficient medical care, no shelters, no food, or housing. A noted professor from the University of Connecticut, James Downs, claims that tens to hundreds of thousands of slaves perished during the American Civil War, either from disease, starvation, or exposure. He claims further that if these deaths were added to the official Civil War deaths count, the number would surely exceed one million.

New and modernized military technologies also need to be taken into account when studying the horrific death tolls of the American Civil War. As we already mentioned, this conflict was unique in many ways, especially as a turning point between archaic and modern methods of warfare. The archaic aspects were mainly centered on troop movements, tactics, and line battles. These were a dated vestige of the Napoleonic Wars, where soldiers would line up in rows and steadily march on in the face of enemy guns and cannons. In many situations, this tactic was largely suicidal. And when this aspect clashed with modern weaponry, the result was terrifying. New weapons emerged in the American Civil War. Notable was the Minie Ball, a new type of bullet that allowed for a greater range and better accuracy. This meant that enemy soldiers marching in line could be picked off from a greater distance, resulting in massive casualties before the distance would be closed in. Repeating rifles were another new and terrible invention. Revolvers were a novelty and reserved for the officers and generals. They had a high rate of fire, and were deadly in close combat. In the late stages of the war, repeating rifles came into play. Most notable were the Spencer and the Henry Repeating rifles. Lever-operated, these rifles had a never-before-seen rate of fire that proved to be deadly in the aged line warfare of the Civil War.

Undoubtedly the most dreadful of all new weapons in the war was the famed Gatling Gun. The highly effective predecessor of the modern machine gun, this repeating rifle had an incredible rate of fire, and was a deadly thing on the Civil War battlefield. However, it came late to the play - it was only patented in 1862 and not yet well known and established during the Civil War. It was, however, used here for the first time ever. During the Siege of Petersburg, 12 Gatling Guns were purchased by the Union forces and used as a preventive against Confederate assaults. In the trench warfare there, they proved a valuable asset, but their use in the war didn't progress further than that.

As a response to the increasingly high casualties as a result of the dated line warfare, new techniques had to be developed in the field. Trench warfare was one such prevention. Seeing that charging in the open was quite deadly when facing modern guns, the warring parties both adopted use of earthworks, cover, and trenches. Trench warfare was especially prevalent during the Siege of Petersburg.

Either way, we can see that the American Civil War overshadowed the other conflicts of its time. When compared to the American-Mexican War that was fought between 1846 and 1848, the devastation and casualties were incredibly higher. The extent of the conflict came as a shock - not only for the United States - but for the rest of the world as well. And when observed from the modern standpoint, we can quickly understand that the American Civil War laid down the groundwork and gave a glimpse of the future wars of attrition and devastation, most notably the First World War.

"A War Like No Other"
Interesting Facts

There is no doubt that the American Civil War was a true war of firsts. Not only in the field of military innovations, but also in all other aspects - from warfare to social practices. Today, we all know the war for the rise of new, modernized weapons such as the Ironclad, the revolver, the Minie Ball, or the Gatling Gun. But what about those lesser known, hard to find facts? These are equally as important to understand just how gruesome and unique this Civil War was.

One of the first lesser known facts is related to the enlistment age. In modern times, young men and boys are exempt from serving in wars and in armies. But back in the 1860s, this was sadly not the case. Because of this, many boys lost their lives in the fiery fields of battle, inexperienced and way, way too young. In fact, official data tells us that roughly 10,413 Union soldiers were under the age of 18 when enlisting for the war effort. They were usually given unique roles in combat. Many of them ended up as "drummer boys", with many being as young as 10 years old. Drummers marched alongside the infantry into the thick of the battle. What is more, there are many recorded tragic instances of boys of 10, 12, and 14 years dying in battles, for causes about which they likely knew nothing.

Continuing our list of interesting facts, we touch upon the "switching of sides". Interestingly, many soldiers of the Civil War fought both on the Northern and the Southern sides. In fact, of the 1,098 officers that were present in the Union Army at the start of the war, some 286 resigned and joined up with the Confederacy. However, of the initial 15,269 of the Union army on the first day of the war, 26 officially joined the Confederate Army, likely out of personal convictions. However, many more had to switch sides involuntarily: as prisoners of war. Thousands of Confederate soldiers, for example, were captured. As prisoners of war, they were eventually released, only to fight on the Union side. Many did it merely for reasons of safety and survival, and not out of personal convictions and causes. Some estimates propose that some 6,000 Confederates switched sides on a volunteer basis. They were commonly called "Galvanized Yankees", a slur originating from their "changing of colors" (of the uniform). Following the war, these men were shunned and rejected in the South where they originated, forcing them to remain in the North.

One of the interesting facts about the Civil War is related to its last surviving veterans. Did you know that the last surviving Union veteran was Albert Woolson, who died on August 2nd, 1956 at the age of 109. He joined the war in October 1864 at age 17, serving as a drummer boy. The last Confederate veteran was John Salling, who died on March 16th, 1959, at the advanced age of 112. He joined the war in 1862 at age 15, serving in the infantry ranks.

The American Civil War was also amongst the first large conflicts to be thoroughly photographed throughout its duration. Matthew Brady was one of the pioneers of photography in America and alongside his colleagues he made many influential photos of the war. His efforts allowed the carnages of war to be documented for posterity and to be shown to the wider public through the newspapers. This helped increase the public awareness of the injustice and the carnage of war.

However, many of these "interesting" facts are, in-fact, not interesting - but rather very tragic. The American Civil War claimed more lives than any other war that the United States ever participated in. With the combined deaths totalling roughly 620,000, and the final casualty toll exceeding 1 million, this was one of the most destructive wars for America. The total population of America in 1865 was 35.2 million, which means that as much as 3% of the entire population was either wounded or killed in the Civil War. And, sadly, the enemies were not foreigners - but fellow Americans of opposing views.

Aftermath of the War and the Conclusion

In comparison with some other major wars of the 19th century, the American Civil War can be seen as a relatively short engagement, lasting just a bit over four years. However, even in such a short amount of time, it had immense consequences that could be felt for decades to follow. The differences between the North and the South could not be mended and washed off in just four years: even in modern times, they persist in the underlying currents of American society. In the South, the memory of the war prevailed the longest, with many refusing to come to terms with the decisive Union victory. There were numerous cases of Southern men and women, veterans, and landowners committing suicide in the years following the Confederate collapse, simply because they did not acknowledge the Federal rule and victory. In the South, racial segregation and injustic continued for many decades following the Civil War and the persistent efforts by Abraham Lincoln to equalize the races and end slavery. And even though the slavery did end, the racial minorities in the south were greatly targeted and segregated. The core southern states developed a myth of the so-called "Lost Cause of the Confederacy": the prevailing belief by Confederate sympathizers, claiming that the cause of the Confederate States was just, heroic, tragic, and not centered on slavery. In many ways, the myth of the Lost Cause was centered on the preservation of the old traditions of Antebellum South, which were greatly lost following the Civil War. Frequent terms related to the Lost Cause are "Northern Aggression" and "States' Rights".

Still, it was this Lost Cause that further shaped the identity of many generations in the South, up to the present day. Race relations and regional differences were never fully mended in America. In fact, the post war years saw the continued rise of racism in the south, even though the African-Americans were free people. One of the major authors on Civil War history, Alan T. Nolan famously said that the

Lost Cause myth *"facilitated the reunification of the North and the South, excusing the virulent racism of the 19th century, and sacrificing black American progress to white man's reunification"*. Furthermore, he describes the Lost cause as a *"caricature of the truth [that] wholly misrepresents and distorts the facts of the matter"*. Of the foremost authors to formalize the Lost Cause myth were Charles and Mary Beard, whose influential work "The Rise of American Civilization", published in 1927, downplays abolitionism and slavery, and defends the Secession as legal. Their work still remains influential amongst Lost Cause proponents, even though it was abandoned by the authors in the 1940's and dismissed by historians of following decades.

To successfully complete the tragic story of the American Civil War, we had to touch upon all its causes, its rapid course, and consequences it had on the American society and the world as a whole. The conflict was long-coming, and expected by many in the months before it actually began. Slavery, although not the only one, is certainly the biggest cause of the war, directly leading to many other points of conflict. And through slavery, the biggest underlying cause of the war was, in the end - money. Traditions and cultural difference aside, it was money that dictated the movements of armies and the firing of bullets - and the bloodshed of the common man. Because slavery - no matter how morally wrong it is - was directly related to the booming economy of the South in the early 19th century. The chiefly agricultural Southern states relied so much on slavery, to a much, much greater extent than the industrial North. Without the slave workforce, South could not continue to thrive and its survival was directly threatened by the ideas of the abolition of slavery. The so-called "institution of slavery" was solidified especially after Eli Whitney's invention of the *cotton gin*, a crucial machine for the processing of cotton that was invented in the late 1700s. With it, the economy of the "King Cotton", i.e. Antebellum South was shaped for good. And when Lincoln threatened this booming economy, the Southerners were ready to defend it.

Still, it was not solely a matter of money and economy. It was also a matter of rising morality in the American North, of the growing understanding and condemning of the inhuman treatment of African-American slaves. This morality was rooted in Revolutionary America, and became a growing point of contentment in the mid 1800s. As we said before, it gave rise to the Abolitionist movement, one of the major threats to the South's ideals, institutions, and traditions.

Studying the complex image of the pre-Civil War America, we can quickly understand that no matter how hard the politicians (both in the North and in the South) tried to remedy the situation and to solve the problem of slavery, they could not have found a quick and lasting solution. In many ways, war was the one to resolve that conundrum. And with the election of Abraham Lincoln in 1860, the tensions finally reached an all-time high, leading to the inevitable Secession of the Southern States and the beginning of the American Civil War. The political leadership, but also the people themselves, thought that the war would end in one direct conflict, but the war lasted for four long years and caused numerous casualties.

When observing the flow of the war, we can see from the start the advantages and disadvantages that both warring factions had. The Confederate South had a clear upper hand in the war's opening stages: it was *on the defensive*. Headed by the highly competent and lauded Robert E. Lee, the South managed to strike a few key victories in the early war. The Union, on the other hand, was in a more difficult position early on. Lincoln was still actively searching for a competent and seasoned military commander, replacing many leaders early on. The situation was greatly remedied only with the rise of Major General Ulysses S. Grant, whose successes and string of victories greatly turned the tide of the war. Grant was competent with his decisive offensive, relentlessness in the field of battle, and his skillful maneuvers. He came to be highly respected both by his allies as well as his enemies. For example, during the Battle of the Wilderness, Robert E. Lee was informed that Grant was retreating. Lee dismissed the information, stating: *"You are mistaken, quite mistaken. Grant is not retreating. He is not a retreating man."*

One of his allies, Colonel Lyman, describes him as such: *"Grant is a man of a good deal of rough dignity; rather taciturn; quick and decided in speech. He habitually wears an expression as if he had determined to drive his head through a brick wall, and was about to do it. I have much confidence in him."*

Undoubtedly, Grant's quick rise to command was the deciding aspect of the Civil War. His relentless pursuit of Robert E. Lee in the Overland Campaign was unlike anything seen before that.

The American Civil War is - for many - a conundrum of the near modern times. No matter how brutal, bloody, and costly in lives - it was a war led for morally good reasons. And, as we all know, no war can be good or lauded or approved of. Because in the very end, it is the innocent men and women and children that perish in the whirlwind of conflicts. But the American Civil War was special. It was fought with the ultimate goal of freeing some four million African-American slaves, ending slavery, and allowing equal voting rights to all citizens. The ultimate price of that moral goal? More than a million lives lost.

Still, to reach freedom, one often has to pass through turmoil and difficulties, bloodshed and grueling warfare.

In the end, all we can do is be thankful for the victims and for the fallen fighters, no matter the side they fought on. For each one fell in the field of battle for a greater cause, and for a unified and determined future of the United States of America. How that future unfolded is a tale for another time.

References:

Cook, R. 2014. *Civil War America: Making a Nation, 1848-1877.* Routledge.

Dean, A. S. 2019. *The Cambridge History of the American Civil War.* Cambridge University Press.

Farmer, A. 2008. *The American Civil War: Causes, Course and Consequences 1803–77.* Hodder Education.

Grant, S. 2014. *The War for a Nation: The American Civil War.* Routledge.

Haramina, I. 2020. *Američki građanski rat 1861. - 1863.* University of Zagreb.

Jurišić, K. 2020. *Američki građanski rat - uzroci, tijek i posljedice.* University of Zagreb, Faculty of Croatian Studies.

Katcher, P. 1995. *The American Civil War Source Book.* Arms and Armour.

Kingseed, C. C. 2004. *The American Civil War.* Greenwood Publishing Group.

Korn, B. W. 1961. *Jews and Negro Slavery in the Old South, 1789-1865.* The Johns Hopkins University Press.

Marinčić, P. 2011. *Američki građanski rat - krvava borba za slobodu.* Essehist.

Meyers, D. J. 2005. *And the War Came: The Slavery Quarrel and the American Civil War.* Algora Publishing.

Mitchell, R. 2013. *The American Civil War, 1861-1865.* Routledge.

Pavelić, M. 2015. *Konfederacija u Američkom građanskom ratu (1861.- 1865.).* Josip Juraj Strossmayer University of Osijek.

Phillips, D. L. 1996. *Civil War Chronicles: Crucial Land Battles.* Metro Books.

Price, H. W. 1961. *Civil War Handbook.* L. B. Prince Co.

Reid, H. B. 2014. *The Origins of the American Civil War.* Routledge.

Tulloch, H. 2006. *The Routledge Companion to the American Civil War Era*. Routledge.

Unknown. 2010. *American Civil War 1861-1865*. Museum of World Treasures.

Various. 2015. *Civil War: A Visual History*. DK Smithsonian.

Various. 2021. *The Story of the American Civil War*. Future Publishing Limited.

Wallenfeldt, J. 2009. *The American Civil War and Reconstruction: People, Politics, and Power*. The Rosen Publishing Group.

Waugh, J. C. 2009. *One Man Great Enough: Abraham Lincoln's Road to Civil War*. HMH.

Wolseley, G. 2002. *The American Civil War: An English View*. Stackpole Books.

Don't miss out!

Visit the website below and you can sign up to receive emails whenever History Nerds publishes a new book. There's no charge and no obligation.

https://books2read.com/r/B-A-ODOK-QKHWB

BOOKS 2 READ

Connecting independent readers to independent writers.

Also by History Nerds

Celtic History
Ireland

Great Wars of the World
World War 1
World War 2
The Napoleonic Wars: One Shot at Glory
The Serbian Revolution: 1804-1835
Peace Won by the Saber: The Crimean War, 1853-1856
The Wars of the Roses

Irish Heroes
Grace O'Malley: The Pirate Queen of Ireland
William Butler Yeats: Nobel Prize Winning Poet
Scáthach
Finn McCool

The History of the Vikings

Vikings
Longships on Restless Seas

The Rise and Fall of Empires
Rome: The Rise and Fall

Standalone
The History of the United Kingdom
The History of Ireland
The History of America
Stalin
The Fiery Maelstrom of Freedom
The History of Scotland
Robert the Bruce
William Wallace: Scotland's Great Freedom Fighter
The History of Wales